PSI AND THE MIND

AN INFORMATION PROCESSING APPROACH

H· J· IRWIN

The Scarecrow Press, Inc.
Metuchen, N.J., & London
1979

Library of Congress Cataloging in Publication Data

Irwin, Harvey J
   Psi and the mind.

   Bibliography: p.
   Includes indexes.
   1. Extrasensory perception. 2. Psychokinesis.
3. Human information processing. I. Title.
BF1321.I78   133.8   79-20587
ISBN 0-8108-1258-4

CONTENTS

PREFACE

but worth reading anyway

This book pursues an account of the experiential nature of psi phenomena. The two fundamental facets of psi, namely extrasensory perception (ESP) and psychokinesis (PK), are explored in terms of a particular view of the mind known as Information Processing Theory.

In essence this theory models the human mind as a system which processes information; that is, one which may accept inputs, extract information from them in a sequence of specifiable stages, store such information for future reference, and if necessary, act upon the information to generate outputs. The processing system analogy has served psychologists well in their attempts to understand normal (as distinct from paranormal) cognitive behavior. The success of information processing theory in this regard encouraged me to consider its applicability to paranormal phenomena of the mind, that is, to the psi experiences of ESP and PK.

With this as its objective the book begins with a description of the mind from an information-processing viewpoint. Chapters 2 and 3 survey the components and modes of operation of the human information processing system. Here discussion of the model is a little simplistic in that I have chosen to play down, and even ignore, some points of controversy as to the characteristics of certain structures

and processes. At the same time this section of the book is intended
not as an exhaustive assessment of current issues in information processing theory, but rather as a relatively uncomplicated descriptive
statement which will enable the reader to grasp the essentials of the
information processing framework.

It is within this framework that I examine the nature of psi experiences. Chapter 4 considers in fairly broad terms the prima facie
aptness of an information processing approach to ESP. The argument progresses to a more detailed and systematic analysis in Chapter 6, where the possible involvement of individual processing components in ESP is discussed. Psychokinetic phenomena are studied
in Chapter 7. Although the analysis here is restricted by lack of relevant data, the nature of PK is explored in relation to various structures of the human information processing system.

The product of these analyses is an account of psi experiences
that is formulated in terms of particular components of the system.
However, information processing models of ESP and PK must also
evidence cognizance of the manner in which the processing system
functions as a whole. The final chapter concerns those characteristics
of psi phenomena that may reflect certain holistic principles governing the operation of the human information processing system.

The critical thesis of this book is that an information processing
approach to psi phenomena is indeed viable. This has a number of
significant implications. Firstly, it constitutes an increase in the explanatory power of information processing theory: that is, the theory
is now seen to be relevant to a wider range of cognitive behavior.
Secondly, information processing models of psi experiences may
provide a valuable context within which future parapsychological re-

search can be conducted. Since few theories in parapsychology have been particularly productive in this regard, such an achievement would be all the more notable. Further, since information processing models of ESP and PK are based on an independently substantiated theory of mind, a critical reassessment of current parapsychological theories may be called for.

The major part of the book was written during a period of sabbatical leave, from February to June 1978. Thanks are due to the Council of the University of New England, New South Wales, for granting this leave. Some sections of the book were initiated before this period. In particular, earlier versions of Chapters 4 and 8 appeared in the *Journal of the American Society for Psychical Research* (see Irwin, 1978a, 1978c). I wish to thank the *Journal*'s editor, Laura A. Dale, and the anonymous reviewers of these papers for their encouragement of my exploration of the information processing approach to psi experiences.

Many of the ideas expounded in the book have been presented in a course, Human Information Processing, which I conduct at the University of New England. During this lecture program my students have provided invaluable criticism and comment which have helped to make the book more comprehensible. For this contribution I hereby give due acknowledgment.

A book such as this can not be written without extensive research. For their assistance in this regard special thanks are due to two groups of people. Firstly the staff of the inter-library loans section of the Dixson Library, University of New England, have been most helpful in locating and borrowing books and journals that I needed for study. Additionally I wish to tender my appreciation to the staff of the Society for Psychical Research, and in particular to Miss Eleanor O'Keeffe, for facilitating my most productive use of material in the Society's library in London during my sabbatical leave this year.

General acknowledgment must be given also to the psychologists and parapsychologists, too numerous to mention here by name, who provided the intellectual stimulation necessary for the conception and execution of the book. Through conversation and correspondence they contributed substantially to the refinement of my ideas.

Finally I must record the valuable role played by my colleagues in the Department of Psychology, University of New England, and by all members of my family. Their general support, encouragement, patience, and good humor were particularly appreciated during the period in which this book was written.

H. J. I.

Department of Psychology,
University of New England,
Armidale, N.S.W., Australia.
October, 1978.

Chapter 1

PSI AND THE MIND

In an overnight train bound for London a Mr. J. Pike found himself alone in his compartment and took the opportunity to stretch out on the seat for a sleep. Early next morning as the train neared its destination he was abruptly shaken awake by the guard. When his mind cleared Pike realized that he had been having a particularly vivid dream. In the dream Pike was dressing in his bedroom at home and twice called his servant by name to request some hot water. It was at this point of the dream that Pike awoke.

On arriving home he learnt that the servant had in fact "heard" Pike calling her twice by name and that, forgetting her master was away from home, she had actually run upstairs in response to the call. This incident occurred at the very time Pike had been dreaming. It may be noted that the details of the servant's experience were known to other members of the family before Pike arrived home and described his dream: this point was independently corroborated by Pike's daughter (Gurney, Myers, and Podmore, 1886, p. 105).

If the facts of Pike's story are accurate (and investigators devoted a deal of effort to ensure authenticity), this case is an example of *telepathy*, that is, apparent communication of information from one mind to another by nonsensory means. Incredible as the above case might seem to some readers, telepathy is hardly a rare phenomenon and well-attested reports of this type abound in the literature. It would seem that the experience of Pike's servant was in the nature of an auditory hallucination. Other reported cases indicate that the spontaneous telepathic experience can take the form of a hallucination in any one or more sensory modalities, dreams, or rather more formless intuitions.

Telepathy is one facet of a broader phenomenon known as extrasensory perception (ESP), which may be defined as the apparent acquisition of noninferential knowledge or information by means that do not involve any of the known senses. Hence, for example, while the experience of Pike's servant was of an auditory type, the information clearly was not received through her ears.

Another proposed variety of ESP is *clairvoyance*. This is akin to telepathy but does not depend on the apparent mediation of another mind. That is, clairvoyance entails extrasensory apprehension of information direct from an object or objective event. In many cases of spontaneous ESP, however, it is difficult to determine whether the percipient's experience is best classified as telepathic or as clairvoyant. An illustrative example may be cited from the file of cases I have gathered from individuals in Australia. Mrs. G (a lady in her sixties) and her sister were accustomed to being regularly taken out for a drive and lunch by a family friend. On one particular day her friend was due to call and Mrs. G took a last look in the mirror to check her appearance. Despite feeling happy and looking forward to the outing, Mrs. G saw in the mirror that she was on the verge of crying: her bottom lip was trembling and tears began to well in her eyes. There was no immediately evident reason for such a reaction. However, Mrs. G's friend failed to keep his appointment, and it was learned subsequently that he had died that same day.

Does this incident constitute a telepathic experience, or a clairvoyant one? Did Mrs. G establish telepathic contact with the mind of her friend just before his death? If a discarnate mind survives bodily death, could telepathy have occurred posthumously? Or was the demise of Mrs. G's friend perceived clairvoyantly by her, that is, as an extrasensorily perceived physical rather than mental event? It is impossible to say. The problem here is not merely one of inadequate information about the experience, but rather that it may be impossible *in principle* to distinguish between telepathy and clairvoyance in many cases of spontaneous ESP. In the present state of knowledge it is as much as we can do to ensure that a given report in all probability represents a genuine instance of ESP.

One further feature of Mrs. G's case warrants acknowledgment. Accepting the experience at face value, the extrasensory information of which the subject was aware is quite limited in this case. While some connotative or affective information about her friend's death appears to have reached consciousness, this certainly did not happen with denotative aspects of the extrasensory information. On bases such as these it is commonly argued that ESP essentially occurs below the level of consciousness and that information admitted to consciousness frequently may be an incomplete and somewhat imprecise characterization of the event from which it presumably derived.

In telepathy and clairvoyance extrasensory information generally corresponds to a contemporaneous event. However, other spontaneous cases suggest that ESP is not restricted by time. Consider the following example from my collection. As a teenager Mrs. L experienced a vision which in some way she knew would be meaningful to her in the future. In the vision Mrs. L lived in a house with a white picket fence and was driving an expensive car to an airport to pick up a man (whom she presumed to be her future husband). At the airport the man came out of an office containing plans or blueprints of some sort. A few years ago Mrs. L was recalling and discussing some of her dreams when she suddenly realized that indeed her vision had been fulfilled. She now does live in a house with a white fence and for many years has been driving her pilot husband to the airport in a beautiful car. The significance of the plans or blueprints in the vision is not yet clear: Mrs. L suggests that perhaps they were meteorological charts which her husband inspects before each flight.

Here, then, Mrs. L extrasensorily acquired information about the future. This type of ESP is termed *precognition.* In the case just cited the precognized event occurred some years after the experience. There is some suggestion that the period between a precognitive experience and its fulfilment is more typically less than two to three days (Orme, 1974; Persinger, 1974, p. 137). Nevertheless the comparative rarity of reported cases in which fulfilment is greatly delayed might be due more to forgetting the original experience than to any temporal property of precognition itself.

It may also be possible for ESP to concern events that have happened in the past. This phenomenon is known as *retrocognition.* Of all the proposed varieties of ESP, retrocognition has the most controversial and equivocal status. In order to authenticate a retrocognitive experience there must be an independent record or memory of the event against which the subject's experience can be checked. It is in the existence of such records that the difficulty lies, since it is not yet possible to determine whether the individual genuinely made extrasensory contact with the past, or unknowingly employed extrasensory information from the records and memories of the event as a basis for the experience. *I have all 3.*

Telepathy, clairvoyance, precognition, and retrocognition are the basic mental or cognitive experiences that comprise the phenomena of ESP. In addition to these, certain paranormal phenomena of a physical nature are known to occur without recognized mechanical causes. Thus there is evidence that individuals can influence the position or structure of objects by means other than use of the known muscular effectors. This nonmechanical, "mind over matter" effect is termed *psychokinesis* (PK). In one of my case studies Mrs. Z reports that on the day her grandmother died there were three knocks on the door of Mrs. Z's flat. On answering the door she found no one there. This continued intermittently for several hours. On the same day a particular cupboard door swung open on a number of occasions, yet the lock did not seem to be malfunctioning. Later that night Mrs. Z and her husband were disturbed by a series of knocks, rattles, and scraping sounds. It was subsequently learned that Mrs. Z's grandmother had died that day. Mrs. Z claims that she was not aware of the imminence of her grandmother's death.

Both animate and inanimate objects may be subject to physical effects of paranormal origin. In spontaneous cases where people have been affected, the basis of the phenomenon is often ambiguous. Thus the individual's physical symptom may reflect a psychokinetic influence or it may constitute a sensory hallucination in response to extrasensorily acquired information. Another incident involving Mrs. Z illustrates this point. At school one day Mrs. Z's daughter gashed her hand on the point of a pair of compasses, and at that precise moment Mrs. Z felt a sharp pain in her hand. Was Mrs. Z's pain caused psychokinetically, or was it a tactile hallucination based on subconscious ESP between mother and daughter? Schwarz (1967) has raised the latter view as a possible account of such phenomena and refers to them as telesomatic reactions. In practice, however, we are usually unable to reliably distinguish between telesomatic reactions and psychokinetic effects on living tissue.

There are many other difficulties in classifying spontaneous cases as unequivocal instances of any given paranormal phenomenon. For example, an ostensible case of telepathy or clairvoyance might equally well be described as evidencing a response whose accuracy the subject has determined by precognition of its subsequent verification. Similarly in certain cases of precognition it might be plausible to argue that the percipient actually causes the occurrence of the "precognized" event through psychokinetic means. For this reason it is appropriate to employ a broad descriptive term collectively designating experiences of general ESP and PK. In the most widely accepted nomenclature today, these effects are known generically as *psi phenomena*. Thus psi phenomena are paranormal effects whose occurrence is in some way dependent on the mind. Scientific investigation of psi phenomena is the subject matter of *parapsychology*.

At the same time *psi* is regarded as more than a blanket term of convenience. That is, its function is not merely to cover a diversity of paranormal events, but to carry the conviction of many parapsychologists that these events share a common phenomenal dimension. The unknown paranormal element that is thought to be a feature of both ESP and PK is represented by the Greek letter ψ ("psi"). To a degree this is done in much the same manner as the algebraist labels his unknown with the letter x until such time as its identity is determined.

Nevertheless the nature of psi is not totally unsuspected. At least it is generally regarded as being critically dependent upon the mind for its expression. Thus relatively few parapsychologists see psi simply as a property of matter, and the possibility of a psychic relationship between two inanimate objects is rarely countenanced. To understand psi phenomena we must therefore understand the nature of mind. It is to this fundamental and significant issue that I address this book.

Admittedly such an objective is by no means novel. There have been many attempts in parapsychology to integrate the properties of psi phenomena with concepts of mind. By and large, however, these efforts have had an essentially philosophical orientation and have argued from the phenomena to a particular theory of mind. The approach I shall adopt here differs from most earlier work in two basic respects. Firstly the view of mind expounded in this book is principally of a psychological rather than philosophical ilk. It is a view derived from psychologists' experimental investigations of normal (as distinct from paranormal) human cognitive behavior. Secondly, instead of considering the characteristics of psi phenomena and then suggesting a theory of mind which can accommodate such characteristics, I will take an established model of the mind and explore the possibility of incorporating psi phenomena into this model.

What then is this particular view of mind, and upon what grounds may its applicability to parapsychological concerns be proposed for analysis? The relevant area of psychological endeavor is known formally

as *information processing theory*. Under this approach the mind is
modeled as a system which processes information; that is, one which
accepts inputs, extracts information from them in a sequence of specifiable stages, stores such information for future reference, and if necessary, acts upon the information to generate outputs. Instead of speaking of the "mind," many psychologists now refer to the *human information processing system*. One of the subsidiary advantages of the
latter term is that it avoids the metaphysical overtones invariably associated with "mind." This is not to say, of course, that the mind is
nothing more than a processor of information; psychologists are merely
looking at the mind from one of many possible perspectives.

It might be asked whether the human information processing system is in fact a model of the mind, or instead models the brain or
central nervous system. Well, there has been much philosophical
speculation on the relationship between mind and brain, and a number
of rival conceptualizations of this relationship have been formulated
over the ages. As far as cognitive psychologists are concerned, however, this issue is not of primary significance. As a group they do not
tend to adopt any one particular view of the mind-brain relationship,
and they are able to proceed with their research without making any
explicit assumptions about this issue. Indeed some "human information processing" psychologists regard the issue as fundamentally ir-
resolvable and see information processing theory as a means of attacking basic questions on cognitive behavior without becoming enmeshed
in the problem of whether the phenomena being studied are those of
the mind or those of the brain. In general it is fair to say that cognitive
psychologists simply seek evidence of processes that the individual
applies to inputs. It is of no particular consequence whether this evi-

dence relates to neurophysiological functions or is in terms of mental operations. The view taken here is that the human information processing system is a model of the mind, or at the very least, of a major facet of the mind. Certain processes of this system may have neuro-physiological correlates (John and Schwartz, 1978), but the matter of how brain and mind are related need not concern us.

Evidence has been derived for a number of specific processes in the human information processing system. The nature of these processes and their role in cognitive aspects of human behavior will be discussed at length in Chapters 2 and 3. Nevertheless it is useful to begin with a cursory outline of the system, since an appreciation of the gross structure of the system will facilitate comprehension of the details of individual processing functions.

A diagrammatic representation of the human information processing system is shown in Figure 1. Each of the identified components of information processing is indicated by a separate element in the diagram. In terms of Figure 1 it is appropriate to speak of the components of the system in spatial terms. Thus each component is referred to as a *processing locus.* Further, processing loci that are involved at an early stage of information processing are designated *low level processes* and are depicted towards the bottom of the diagram. Subsequent, typically more sophisticated, processes are achieved by higher level loci represented near the top of Figure 1. Thus processing of a sensory stimulus may be conceived as basically involving a flow of information up through the human information processing system; that is, from "input" to "output" in the diagram.

The functions of the various processing loci may be briefly defined as follows. The sense organs provide the means by which information

Psi and the Mind

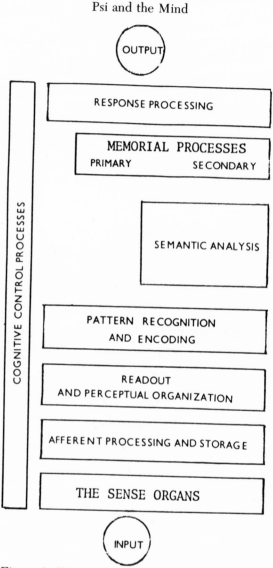

Figure 1. Human Information Processing System.

from the individual's sensory environment may be admitted to the processing system. This sensory information is subject to some preliminary analysis to determine the sensory features present in the input: this phase is known as afferent processing. The sensory features thus identified are stored for a brief period of time in a type of memory, a so-called afferent store. Thus in this store the input is represented as a set of sensory features. Such storage permits further processes to be applied to the information. The stored information is continuously transferred from, or "read out" of, the afferent store and at the same time the information is organized for higher-level processing. Hence at this locus, for example, information about a focal object is distinguished from that about its background. At the next level of processing the information is "recognized," that is, it is compared to and matched against previously experienced inputs. The "recognized" pattern is then put into a form which permits the individual to extract the meaning of the information: these functions are performed respectively by the loci of encoding and semantic analysis.

To this stage of processing, all functions have been carried out below the level of consciousness. The individual therefore is not directly aware of the processes at or below the level of semantic analysis. However, he may become aware of the net *results* of these processes if the information proceeds to the next level of the system, that of memorial processes. At this locus information is further processed so that it may be stored in memory; one of the processes here entails conscious perception of the input. Under certain circumstances it may also be appropriate to respond to the input in some way. Selection of a response and its execution are held to be governed by the locus of response processing. Between the "input" and "output" points of the system, therefore, many distinct processes are applied to sensory information. However, the flow of such information through the system is by no means automatic. At various stages of processing, decisions are required as to how further processing should proceed. This executive control of the system is a function of the locus of cognitive control processes.

The processing system analogy has served psychologists well in their attempts to understand cognitive aspects of human behavior (see, e.g., Haber, 1974; Simon, 1979). The above theoretical framework has provided the foundation of modern approaches to such diverse cognitive phenomena as attention, intelligence, memory, problem solving, and language, as well as elucidating cognitive aspects of individual differences and social interaction. It is becoming increasingly clear that in information processing theory psychologists have a paradigm with wide ecological validity. The success of the model in accounting for normal cognitive phenomena encourages consideration of its applicability to paranormal phenomena of the mind, namely ESP and PK. This issue is critically explored in subsequent chapters.

It is appropriate to indicate the potential value of this exercise. If an acceptable account of psi phenomena can be offered within an information processing framework it may yield a number of dividends. In the first place such an account would further enhance the explanatory power of information processing theory by significantly broadening the range of phenomena to which it is relevant. Secondly, an information processing model of psi could provide a meaningful context within which future parapsychological research may be conducted. At present parapsychology is marked by a dearth of theoretical paradigms that are particularly productive of research. Additionally, if a theory of mind is required for the explanation of psi phenomena, a degree of confidence can be placed in that explanation if the associated theory of mind has been independently documented and empirically substantiated. Formulation of a cogent and viable information processing model of psi would thereby call for critical reassessment of alternative theories in this field.

Nevertheless it remains to be shown whether or not psi phenomena can be meaningfully formulated in information processing terms. To this end the remainder of the book is organized along the following lines. In Chapters 2 and 3 the nature of the human information processing system is thoroughly reviewed, both in terms of the functions of individual processing loci and in relation to the operation of the system as a whole. The basis of an information processing model of ESP is explored in the three subsequent chapters: various potential models are discussed and evaluated in the light of empirical data on the involvement of particular processing loci in ESP. In Chapter 7 the phenomenon of psychokinesis is subject to a similar analysis. The concluding chapter is devoted to the relationship between psi phenomena and principles which govern the global operation of the human information processing system.

Chapter 2

COMPONENTS OF THE
HUMAN INFORMATION PROCESSING SYSTEM

In their investigation of the mind from the information processing approach, psychologists have derived empirical evidence for a number of specific processing mechanisms or loci. Further research has established in more detail the processing characteristics of these loci, and it is to a review of such characteristics that we now turn. An understanding of the nature of each component is essential to an appreciation of the system's operation as a whole.

The following discussion of each processing locus is keyed to the diagrammatic representation of the human information processing system in Figure 1. Throughout the review in this chapter it is assumed that the information with which each component is dealing relates to an environmental stimulus received by the system in a normal rather than paranormal manner.

Cognitive Control Processes

It is becoming increasingly recognized that there is a certain amount of flexibility in the flow and sequencing of information in the processing system. To take account of this it is hypothesized that the progression of information through the processing system is governed by *cognitive control processes*. This concept was originally introduced in the context of memory systems (Atkinson and Shiffrin, 1968) and is now extended to the information processing system as a whole.

Cognitive control processes regulate information flow by operating at points of decision in the system. The nature of decisions required at each processing locus will be described in subsequent sections of this chapter. At the present point it is sufficient to note that the postulated operation of control decisions is based upon the tenet that cognition is an active rather than passive affair. It is thus inappropriate to conceive of the human information processing system as a perceptual drainage complex, with rigidly defined channels along which sensory inputs automatically stream. Rather there is a measure of flexibility in the way in which the system can deal with information. A given input may receive merely superficial analysis at a given locus, or its processing may be assiduous and comprehensive. The input may be processed in an orderly linear fashion as it progresses up the system, or its analysis at lower loci may be affected by expectations of the nature of its informational content at higher loci. It may be fully dealt with at one locus before proceeding to the next, or before such processing is complete partial information about the nature of the input may be used to initiate processing at the next locus. The information may be permitted access to consciousness, or we may remain unaware of it. There are many ways in which the progress of an input through the human information processing system is subject to variation. Determination and coordination of information flow are executive functions served by the locus of control processes.

Additionally cognitive control processes are involved in systemic functions that follow receptive analysis of an input. They may govern selection of a response to the input, or guide retrieval of information from memory. The individual can be aware of applying control processes at some loci of the system. In many instances, however, these executive decisions are made at *preconscious* levels of processing, and we can be aware only of the net outcome of a series of such decisions.

Control processes therefore reflect the labile processing strategies which are adopted by the individual (consciously or otherwise) in accordance with past experience and the cognitive demands of the current situation. These executive processes are applied at points of decision in the system, that is, at loci where an assessment must be made as to the most appropriate way to proceed with processing.

The Sense Organs

Ignoring for now the possibility of extrasensory perception, the sense organs constitute the means by which environmental information may enter the processing system. The diversity of man's sense organs reflects the variety of information in the environment that is potentially relevant to his survival. Among our generally recognized senses are those of vision, hearing, smell, taste, touch, balance, and bodily movement. At the same time, in spite of this variety of sensory information receptors, there is much information in the environment to which humans are insensitive. For example there is "light" we cannot see, "sounds" we cannot hear: that these exist is known from artificial sensors of electromagnetic radiation and from behaviorally-evidenced sensory abilities of other animals. Additionally, as yet undiscovered forms of energy may exist. In this respect, then, our sense organs provide us with a rather limited sample of the information that is available in our environment.

The sensory information admitted to the processing system is also restricted by selective adjustment of the sense organs and associated peripheral systems. This is especially the case with the dominant sensory modality in humans, vision. By selective movement of the eyes, eyelids, head, and body, visual information can be either admitted to or excluded from the processing system. Such movements depend on informational feedback from higher processing loci. In other words, at higher levels of the system an assessment is made as to whether the currently most relevant visual input is stimulating the most sensitive part of the retina of the eye, or is falling instead in its less sensitive periphery. On the basis of this assessment and concomitant cognitive control decisions, the orientation of the eyes is accordingly adjusted. Other feedback processes ensure that the retinal image is in focus and has suitable depth of field. These adjustments proceed constantly, with the result that extraction of relevant visual information is as efficient as possible. At the other extreme, highly undesirable or unpleasant visual stimuli in the environment can be excluded from the processing system if the individual simply looks away or closes his eyes. Therefore in vision, and to a less extent in other sensory modalities, selection of input to the human information processing system is achieved to some degree at the level of the sense organs, with control processes serving a mediational role.

The sense organs also represent the first stage of the system at which stimulus information is *encoded*, that is, where a qualitative change occurs in the form of the information. As a sensory input, stimulus information is comprised of a particular set of values on a number of dimensions of physical energy, such as intensity and wavelength (spectrum). It is the function of sense organs to register information represented in physical terms and to translate it into information coded by neural impulses. This process is termed sensory transduction. The purpose of encoding (at this and any other loci of the system) is to put information in a form that is appropriate for its subsequent processing.

Afferent Processing and Afferent Storage

After being registered by the appropriate sense organ the input's sensory or *afferent* characteristics are extracted. This is achieved by certain feature-detection processes which are the basis for organization of the receptive field. The nature of afferent processing is best documented for the modality of vision. In this case the primitive features thus identified include lines, angles, edges, length, size, orientation, velocity, color, and retinal disparity. Thus at this locus of processing the presence of such features in the visual input is determined. There is a good deal of neurophysiological evidence for visual feature-detection processes, and some for afferent processing of auditory features (see Lindsay and Norman, 1977, pp. 230–251 for a review).

It must be emphasized that processes at this locus of the system are preconscious. The individual is not aware of the operation of feature detectors. Consciousness is identified with a much higher locus of the processing system: afferent processing is simply one of several low-level functions that are entailed in mediating sensory information to this higher locus.

The preconscious nature of feature detection may be illustrated by reference to a particular type of brain disorder; this example should also encourage greater appreciation of the role of feature detection in cognition. The disorder with which we are concerned has the paradoxical name of "blind sight." A patient suffering this condition is for all practical purposes blind. He reports absence of any conscious visual experience, and is unable to identify objects or to find his way about the environment by visual means. However, a curious effect occurs with such an individual in the laboratory (Weiskrantz, Warrington, Sanders, and Marshall, 1974). The patient is presented with a slit of light in an otherwise darkened room, and is asked to report whether the slit of light is vertical or horizontal. He initially objects that he can not see anything at all, but eventually agrees to play the experimenter's "game" by guessing at the line's orientation. When he does so it is with surprisingly high accuracy, although he continues to maintain that he is merely guessing. Similar effects are found in "guessing" whether a given letter is an X or an O. It appears that in blind sight certain visual feature detectors are intact and respond normally to visual input. At some higher level of the system, however, there is evidently some defect which prevents the results of afferent processing from being integrated or otherwise utilized as a basis for conscious visual experience.

At the locus of afferent processing, therefore, input is encoded in terms of its primitive sensory features. An important facet of the human information processing system is that this afferent information may be stored for a brief period. This provides the opportunity for higher processes to be applied to information extracted from the stimulus array. The duration of afferent storage is a critical parameter in this regard: it must be sufficient for higher processes to be completed, but not so long as to interfere with storage of subsequent inputs.

The duration of afferent storage varies with the modality of the input. On this and other grounds it is argued that there is a different afferent store corresponding to each sensory modality. Thus visual input is held in an *iconic store* and auditory input in an *echoic store* (Neisser, 1967). Afferent storage of information in other modalities is not well researched, although there is some evidence of an afferent store for tactile inputs (e.g., Bliss, Crane, Mansfield and Townsend, 1966).

The capacity of afferent stores is substantial. Sperling (1963) has shown that the iconic store can hold at least 17 of 18 letters presented in three rows of six. However, the iconic store should not be regarded as a veridical, "photographic" representation of the stimulus, but rather a very rich store of the primitive visual features extracted from the stimulus. Nevertheless afferent stores do hold relatively untransformed information: their contents are certainly not integrated or classified according to meaning. At this level of processing, input is still unidentified and unrecognized. For this reason some psychologists describe afferent storage as "precategorical."

The time course of afferent storage can best be exemplified in relation to the iconic store. Iconic representation of an input is established soon after stimulus onset and continues while the retinal image remains unchanged. When the input is either terminated or changed, its iconic representation persists but rapidly evanesces, loses fidelity, or "decays." Thus for a limited time after stimulus offset, information about the input is available for further analysis. The post-offset period in which this afferent visual information may be utilized is typically found to be about a quarter of a second, although this varies with such factors as the luminance and duration of the stimulus, the extent to which the eye is dark adapted, and the nature of the input that follows stimulus exposure.

Echoic memory is characterized by a similar time course, except that the duration of echoic representation after stimulus offset is generally estimated at four to six seconds. This period is considerably longer than that for iconic storage, presumably because auditory cognition, particularly in the case of speech, is heavily dependent on integration of information over time.

It is not yet clear if feature detectors extract information which is then represented in an afferent store: it is possible that these processes are concurrent. Sakitt (1976) has reported some data which suggest that visual feature detection actually occurs in the iconic store rather than prior to admission to this store. Further research is being conducted on this issue (e.g., by Banks and Barber, 1977; McCloskey and Watkins, 1978). In Figure 1 afferent processing and afferent storage are shown in the same section of the diagram to indicate that these functions are realized in at least the same general *region* of the processing system.

Readout and Perceptual Organization

For the period in which it is held in an afferent store, stimulus information is continuously transferred to the next stages of processing, namely, pattern recognition and input encoding. This transference of information is called *readout,* although this term is perhaps more suited to describing transfer from the iconic store than that from afferent stores in nonvisual modalities. In the course of readout, information is also *organized* for subsequent processing: for example, at this level the distinction between figure and ground is established. This aspect of readout is known as perceptual organization.

There is some degree of flexibility in perceptual organization, that is, through selective application of cognitive control processes, afferent information may be differentially organized for subsequent analysis. The term *selective readout* refers to the situation in which specific strategies are employed in organizational processes at this level of the system. Such strategies are successful where they are based upon primitive sensory features, that is, upon the form in which information is coded at this stage of processing. For example, in readout from the iconic store it is possible to differentially organize information in terms of its location, color, brightness, shape, and size (e.g., Sperling, 1960; von Wright, 1970). However, perceptual organization at this level of the processing system is not possible for semantically defined cues: selective readout can not be based on the distinction between vowels and consonants, for example (von Wright, 1970). This emphasizes the point that items in afferent stores have yet to be identified as previously experienced patterns and to be analysed for meaning; as a consequence selection cues not based on primitive sensory features are unefficacious in readout.

At the same time it is not essential to employ intentional strategies in readout, as perceptual organization can be achieved without the involvement of control processes. In *nonselective readout* organization of afferent information is achieved through automatic operation of the Gestalt laws of perceptual grouping and figure-ground segregation (see Wertheimer, 1958). There is also some evidence that, at least with alphabetic material, information in a visual display is organized for subsequent processing in a left-to-right, top-to-bottom order (Dick, 1971; Mewhort, Merikle and Bryden, 1969).

Irrespective of the type of readout, perceptual organization at this level achieves differentiation of *figure* and *ground*. This may be illustrated by way of a simple exercise. Rapidly scan down your bookshelves until you find a volume with a red cover. You will find that the red book seems to "stand out" from others in your bookcase, with non-red books appearing as nondescript background. Again it should be emphasized that this is not due to any difference between the extraction of "figure" information from afferent stores and that of "ground" information. The effect stems from the *organization* of figure and ground for differential processing at higher loci.

Pattern Recognition and Input Encoding

Stimulus information is represented in afferent stores in terms of its primitive sensory features. When this information is read out of an afferent store the coded features are combined or synthesized according to their consistency with familiar patterns. This preconscious process is known as *pattern recognition,* and it involves detection of critical features which identify the input as a previously experienced pattern. For example, in the case of a visual display, critical afferent features will identify one configuration as the letter "B" and another as rectangular. Various levels of afferent features may be utilized here. Thus in word recognition, information relating to individual letters and groups of letters is typically used in conjunction with holistic information about the word, such as its length and shape.

Pattern recognition is another process characterized by some flexibility. One such function at this locus is the transformation of extracted information in order that it may be recognized. Hence a B rotated through 90 degrees or a rectangle sloping away from the observer can still be correctly identified. Additionally, there is flexibility in effecting a choice among alternatives that are activated. For example, the set of critical visual features for B and that for 8 would overlap to some extent, and consequently selection of one in preference to the other will be necessary when one of these characters is the stimulus item. The choice among alternative patterns is markedly affected by sets, expectations and contexts. Thus in the above example the pattern "8" may be selected if the observer is expecting to see a digit, and "B" if a letter is expected. Control processes may be called upon in effecting such a choice.

This example also illustrates the point that a pattern need not have all the critical features for "recognition" to occur. In the first place recognition can be successfully based on partial identification of critical features supplemented with contextual information. Hence in reading prose we do not need to detect and identify every feature of eviry letter of every word: the typographical error in this sentence probably went unnoticed in your initial reading, and it should not have affected your comprehension of the sentence. Further, with "noise" from various sources in the system interfering with processing, information extraction simply can not be perfectly efficient or veridical on all occasions. At the locus of pattern recognition, therefore, the processing system must take the "best bet" as to the identity of an input, and continue to process the information under this assumption until some contradiction or inconsistency becomes evident.

It should also be noted that the sensory features of an input are not all of equal importance in pattern recognition. For example, in recognizing a face the region of the eyes is of particular significance: you will have noted how difficult it can be to recognize someone who is wearing dark glasses. Pattern recognition is therefore a product of differential weighting of critical afferent features.

The role of detection of critical features in pattern recognition can be demonstrated through a short exercise. Start at the top of the first list of letters below and scan down it as quickly as you can until you find the letter T. Then repeat the task for the second list.

MFVZ	GQRO
XHEL	BUCS
NIWF	UPQG
ZKYH	SCOD
VFIW	RQCU
EYML	OUPQ
HNZK	QBSC
IVMF	DCUO
WLTY	SOGR
FKXN	UCTQ
YZHE	BGOC

It is typically found that it takes longer to locate the target letter on the first list than on the second. The reason for this should be clear if you have performed the task: the letters in the first list have some of the critical features of the target letter T, whereas this is less the case in the second list. This is a compelling illustration of the dependence of pattern recognition upon critical features.

Given that the duration of afferent storage of information is sufficient, afferent features coded in this store thus provide the basis for preconscious identification of the input with a previously experienced pattern. It should be noted, however, that pattern recognition does not entail determination of the input's meaning. Suppose, for example, that the word TREE was presented visually. In pattern recognition of this information, TREE is identified simply as a word the individual has seen before. On the other hand, precisely what the individual takes this word to mean is a matter for elaboration at a subsequent locus of the system.

Following the processes of pattern recognition the information is recoded into forms appropriate for its semantic analysis and its representation in a store known as primary memory. This function is known as *input encoding*, and entails a further qualitative change in the form of extracted information. Two types of code that may be established at this locus are *visual* and *verbal* codes.

The visual code entails representation of the stimulus information in visuospatial terms; in the case of the verbal code representation takes a phonemic (acoustic and/or articulatory) form. Thus with visual stimuli the visual code will comprise a visuospatial or abstracted "physical" representation of the input, while the verbal code will correspond to the *name* of the input. The formation of these two codes is achieved concurrently or "in parallel" by separate coding systems. It might seem surprising that with visual input, the visual code is not established first and the "name" code derived from this. However, it should be remembered that these codes are based not upon the input as such but upon the results of its pattern recognition. Once the input is identified as a familiar one, the recognized pattern itself can be represented simultaneously in a visual form and by name.

Nevertheless the formation of the two codes does not proceed at the same rate. For visually presented sets of letters it has been suggested that visual encoding occurs at a rate of approximately 10 milliseconds per letter, with a verbal code requiring about 100 milliseconds per letter (Coltheart, 1972). The difference in rate of visual and verbal encoding has been elegantly demonstrated in an experimental paradigm called the *letter matching task* (Posner and Mitchell, 1967). In this task two letters that are either both vowels or both consonants are categorized as of the same class, while a pair with one vowel and one consonant is defined to feature different classes. The subjects in the letter matching task are required to signal as quickly as possible whether two visually presented letters have the same class or whether they differ in class. It is found that reaction time to a stimulus pair like AA is significantly faster than that to a pair like Aa, which in turn is classified more quickly than a pair such as AE. Now, classification of AA as "same" would simply require comparison of the visual codes of the two letters. Classification of Aa as "same" could not be achieved in this way, but could be done by comparing the names (verbal codes) of the letters. Finally, identification of AE as "same" would necessitate some semantic analysis of each letter to determine whether it was a vowel or a consonant. The finding that identification time increased over the three respective types of stimulus items suggests that the visual codes were established more quickly than the verbal codes, while both visual and verbal encoding was faster than semantic analysis.

The dual systems responsible for visual and verbal encoding therefore feature different processing rates. There may also be other differences in the processing characteristics of these coding systems. Coltheart (1972) has suggested that, at least for nonselective readout from the iconic store, visual encoding is more likely for items at the ends of a stimulus display, while verbal coding appears to proceed from items at the left side of the display to those at the right. In any event it is clear that two distinct coding processes may be applied to the information derived from pattern recognition.

Semantic Analysis

The next locus of the human information processing system is concerned with *semantic analysis* of encoded input, that is, the elaboration of its meaning and its associations for the individual.

The distinction between pattern recognition and semantic analysis warrants reiteration. Pattern recognition involves nothing more than a matching of the input with a previously experienced pattern: this must be done before the input can be named (i.e., verbally encoded). Semantic analysis, on the other hand, goes beyond mere matching against a pattern. It relates to the meaning, or meanings, we attach to that pattern, that is, the input's denotative and connotative characteristics.

For some time it was believed that semantic analysis of an input is mediated only by the input's verbal code. That it can be so mediated is unequivocal. For example, consider the following "sentence":

EYE SEA YEW NO WARE TWO REED INN PIECE

Now, each individual word here is a legitimate element of the English language, so there is no problem in pattern recognition of the words. In fact we can actually make sense of the "sentence" if we take particular cognizance of the sounds (verbal codes) of the words. (If you still find it unintelligible, read it aloud.) That we are able to comprehend the material demonstrates the role of the verbal code in mediating semantic analysis. At the same time, however, we do realize that these words do not form a legitimate sentence: when interpreted graphemically rather than phonemically they do not convey any collective meaning (see Baron, 1973). The visual code therefore does play some role in mediating semantic processes. Indeed there is evidence now accumulating that at least under certain circumstances, semantic analysis can be based purely on visually encoded information (see Bradshaw, 1975, for a review).

Apparently, therefore, there is flexibility in the mediation of semantic analysis, with the use of a particular code dependent upon the nature of the processing task. In fact it has been found possible to manipulate the system's relative dependence on visual and verbal codes in mediation of meaning (e.g., see Irwin, 1978b); such manipulation would presumably be effected through control processes.

Semantic analysis of an input involves elaboration of the input's denotative and connotative features. In that this comprises an additional, qualitatively distinct form of input representation, it is appropriate to regard these features as a semantic code of the input. The precise nature of the features comprising the semantic code is still a matter of conjecture. Osgood, Suci and Tannenbaum (1957) have conducted some research on connotative features of words—that is, the types of affective characteristics attributed to the referent of a word. They propose that the connotative nature of such inputs is encoded in the form of representation on three affective dimensions, *evaluation, activity* and *potency*. Evaluation essentially involves the "good-bad" or "pleasant-unpleasant" dimensions; activity relates to "active-passive" or "lively-still"; and potency is a "strong-weak" or "tough-tender" factor. Several further studies have yielded results consistent with this taxonomy of connotative features.

On the other hand it appears that the nature of *denotative* features might not be reduced to such an elegant formulation. It is not even clear at which level of denotative meaning such features should be sought. For example, if you are observing a canary, are denotative features elaborated at the conceptual level of "bird" and "domesticated," or are they more basic, such as "small" and "yellow"? At present, models of denotative coding range from those in which the relationships between denotative dimensions are unspecified (e.g., Underwood, 1969) to models in which such dimensions form a hierarchical structure (e.g., Collins and Quillian, 1972). The nature of the elemental denotative feature will be determined only after considerable further empirical investigation (see Bierwisch, 1971).

A further complication in semantic coding arises when the input is ambiguous. Is one interpretation of the input selected for semantic analysis in such a case, or are both alternative interpretations semantically encoded? It is typically found that when presented with ambiguous information the individual is immediately aware of just a single interpretation. Consider, for example, the sentence "He threw a stone at the bank." Normally readers will have initially assumed *either* that the subject was in the vicinity of a savings institution, *or* that he was near a river. The bases upon which one interpretation is selected for admission to consciousness is not of concern at this point. The fact that such a selection is normally made in the processing system need not, however, imply that only the selected interpretation received preconscious semantic encoding. Conrad (1974) has in fact reported evidence that *both* meanings of an ambiguous input may be simultaneously elaborated at this locus. It is not known if this result may be generalized to semantic coding of inputs having multiple meanings. If all possible meanings of an input are preconsciously elaborated, we can only applaud Humpty Dumpty's practice of paying extra wages to words which have many different interpretations.

At the same time it should be emphasized that not every input receives searching semantic analysis. The extent or "breadth" of semantic coding will depend in part on the importance of other concurrent demands placed upon the processing system (see Chapter 3). If the input is admitted to consciousness the individual may elect to continue its semantic elaboration at the conscious level, or to be more precise, further preconscious semantic encoding may be instituted and the results of this additional processing admitted to consciousness.

On the basis of our own introspective experiences it may seem surprising that the meaning of information can be extracted at anything other than a conscious level. Nevertheless there is evidence from a variety of sources that the meaning of input is processed preconsciously, and that indeed such processing may proceed without an individual's ever becoming aware of the meaning of the input. Readers who wish to pursue the evidence in some detail should examine the literature in the areas of subception, subliminal perception, perceptual defense, and selective attention (Dixon, 1971; Erdelyi, 1974; Lackner and Garrett, 1973; Lazarus and McCleary, 1951).

For present purposes of illustration a study conducted by Worthington (1964) will suffice. In this experiment each subject (a male student) was seated in an artificially illuminated room for a period sufficient to enable his eyes to become adapted to the level of illumination. The lights were then extinguished and the subject was asked to look at a small screen on to which a very dim light was being projected. As the subject's eyes adapted to the dark he eventually became aware of the target light. When he had the faintest impression that the light was present, the subject signalled this information to the experimenter. Now, unknown to the subject, the target actually consisted of a four-letter word projected on the screen. The emotionality of these stimulus words was varied across trials. Some words, such as "tent," were relatively neutral; others, such as "shit," were more emotionally charged. Worthington found that on the average, subjects took around seven seconds longer to report awareness of the target light when this was an emotional word than when it was neutral. At no time, however, did subjects become aware of the meaning of the stimulus word: indeed throughout the experiment they remained ignorant that the target light was actually a word at all. The data of this study therefore demonstrate that at some preconscious level of processing, subjects were able to distinguish between emotional and nonemotional stimuli.

There is also some tentative evidence that different semantic features may be encoded either at different rates or at different stages of semantic processing (Wickens, 1972, pp. 208–212). Interestingly enough, the *unpleasantness* of input is reported to be one of the first semantic features to be extracted. Perhaps this property of semantic encoding reflects some survival value. However, Wickens has indicated (in a personal communication) that he regards

the observed effects as being weak and needful of independent replication.

At this level of processing, therefore, stimulus information is
represented in three distinct forms: a visual code, a verbal code, and
a semantic code. At the same time it should be noted that the
wealth of detail in the semantic code is particularly limited by the
demands of other concurrent processes in the system.

Memorial Processes

Psychologists have distinguished two general classes of processing related to (non-afferent) memory. One class serves "short-term"
purposes and the other, "long-term."

The short-term system of processes is known as *primary memory,* and its function is to effect storage of information that we require to be held only for a short time, ranging from a few seconds to
perhaps a minute or two. For example, after extracting a number
from the telephone directory, you need to retain this information
only for as long as it takes to dial the number and check that you
have been connected to the intended recipient. Similarly, in pur-
chasing goods at the supermarket, until you receive your change you
need to retain the information that you gave the cashier a twenty-
dollar note and not a ten-dollar one. These types of memorial tasks
rely principally on the processes of primary memory. There is also
some consensus of opinion that primary memory represents the seat
of consciousness, that is, the individual becomes aware of information to which the processes of primary memory are applied.

On the other hand there are some pieces of information that we wish to retain for longer periods. These may range from episodes in our personal history, such as the day we started school, to conceptual items, such as our own telephone number or that two times two equals four. The system of processes responsible for long-term storage of this kind is termed *secondary memory*.

One general point must be made on the concept of primary and secondary memory systems. It may well be inappropriate to think of these systems as separate "compartments" in which information is stored for different purposes. At present there is increasing support for the view that the difference between items retrievable in the long term and those available only for short-term recall lies in the *processes* that have been applied to these items; that is, in the depth and exhaustiveness of their analysis (Craik and Lockhart, 1972; Craik and Tulving, 1975; Postman, 1975). It is advisable therefore to distinguish between primary and secondary memory simply in terms of their processing characteristics. Thus primary memory is that aspect of the memory system whereby application of certain processes is associated with conscious perception of the information and its retention for short-term purposes. Secondary memory is a further aspect of the memory system whereby application of (other) processes to the information enhances its retrieval in the long-term. In this regard, then, the expression "admission to primary memory" should be interpreted as an elliptical reference to a procedure of representing an input in the memory system and subjecting this representation to the processes of primary memory.

Following the processes of visual, verbal, and semantic encoding, coded information may be admitted to primary memory and retained in this form for a short period. At any one time the quantity of information that can be held as a primary representation is very limited. In fact the capacity of primary storage varies according to the type of code involved: while primary processes may be applied concurrently to four or five visually coded items, the capacity for verbal codes may extend to eight or more. These estimates are necessarily approximate in that the size of an "item" here depends upon how much information the individual can incorporate in each "chunk." For example, there are many more chunks of information in the letter-string TLPOIHSA than in HOSPITAL, despite the identity of the components of the two strings.

As a consequence of the limited capacity of primary memory, a selection must be made among concurrently encoded items as to which of them will gain access to primary memory. Such selection, presumably the function of a cognitive control process, is thought to be on the basis of the subjective importance of respective inputs. That is, the item which is most relevant to the individual at that time is given priority in admission to primary memory. Davis and Smith (1972), for example, have demonstrated that when subjects are instructed to attend only to one of two simultaneous inputs to the information processing system, the "unattended" inputs are not stored in primary memory. Selection on the basis of relevance would also apply between alternative meanings of an ambiguous input.

Not only the capacity but also the *duration* of primary representation varies across codes. If no further processes are applied to the contents of primary memory, the information quickly decays. The duration of visual codes here is but a few seconds; verbal codes, on the other hand, may survive for about twenty seconds. The dura-

tion of primary storage is further diminished by the effects of interference from items subsequently admitted to the store.

Nevertheless it is possible to maintain primary representation of
an item through application of a control process known technically as
type I rehearsal. This process does not entail any further analysis or
extraction of information from the input, but rather rote repetition
or "recycling" of the information for the purpose of its maintenance.
In this way it is possible to maintain visual codes in primary memory
for nine seconds or more. Verbal codes may be similarly maintained
for extensive periods, limited only by such factors as fatigue and the
need to engage in other cognitive activities. However, type I rehearsal is a time-consuming process, and this necessarily restricts
the amount of information in primary memory that can be maintained in this way.

One further aspect of primary storage of a visual code may be
noted at this point. In the case of a visual input such as a printed
word, the visual code entails a visuospatial representation of the
letter-string rather than of the referent of the word. Nevertheless,
subject to other current processing demands in the system, there
may be some feedback from the level of semantic processing to that
of visual encoding which achieves the formation of a visual code corresponding to the *referent*. One factor in this process is the extent
to which the referent is physical rather than abstract; that is, the establishment of this additional visual code depends upon the referent's *concreteness*. Now, visual coding of the input's referent is
not achieved until a second or more after stimulus onset (Paivio,
1971). In the meantime the visual code corresponding to the input
itself may have decayed to some extent and thereby will have poorer

fidelity than the visual code of the referent. Consequently, if extracted information is to be maintained in primary memory for some time, type I rehearsal may be selectively applied to the visual code of the referent in preference to that of the original input. This may account for Bartram's (1976) observation that with pictorial stimuli, visual codes appear to change over time from veridical "input" representations to more abstracted "referent" representations.

It was mentioned above that primary memory is thought to be the locus of consciousness. This view is based in part on evidence that processes below the level of primary memory can proceed without an individual's necessarily becoming aware of the results of such processes. Beyond this source of support, however, we begin to encounter logical difficulties. The essence of the predicament is that the contents of primary memory are defined empirically as those items which the individual can currently report (or, for which his consciousness can be demonstrated). It is clearly circular to maintain that consciousness consists of the contents of primary memory if the latter can only be defined in terms of the former. At present there seems to be no solution to this dilemma, other than to regard this view of consciousness as axiomatic. In other words, under the information-processing approach the seat of consciousness is taken to be primary memory, and research will proceed on this assumption until the model is demonstrably no longer viable.

The view that consciousness may be identified with just a single locus in the information processing system may also strike some readers as simplistic and incapable of capturing the immense variety of conscious experience. After all, there are considerable differences in the nature of consciousness across such states as "normal" waking awareness, sleep, drug intoxication, meditation, and hypnotic trance. Further, information at the focus of attention is characterized by a qualitatively different state of consciousness than is information in the periphery of attention. How can the operation of one single processing locus accommodate such a wide range of states of consciousness? The answer is that states of consciousness vary in respect to the type of information admitted to primary memory. Under some states, for example, input is thoroughly and extensively encoded before it is perceived; in other states of consciousness, input may be subjected only to very gross and incomplete pattern recognition and encoding. The *nature* of conscious experience is thus very much dependent on processes at loci below the level of primary memory; the systemic site of the experience itself, however, is identified with that locus alone.

Information in memory may be subject to additional processes which will enhance the likelihood of retrieving that information in the long term. The representation of the input as a secondary memory trace is generally described as entailing "transfer" from primary to secondary memory, although this term is not entirely appropriate in that it suggests a spatial distinction between these systems. The control processes for elaborating the encoded information into a secondary memory trace are collectively designated as *type II rehearsal*. This involves organization of the input in relation to other material previously stored in secondary memory. This mediation between the input and other secondary traces entails visual, verbal, and semantic dimensions. Thus type II rehearsal may take the form of a visual image in which two referents are depicted in an associative relationship. Similarly, the association may be encoded through the use of language: to store the number of days in each month of the year we employ the mnemonic, "Thirty days hath September. . . . " Finally, mediation may be by way of semantic associations. Any or all of these mediating processes may be employed to encode the input in a form suitable for long-term retention.

In spite of these diverse processes, however, secondary representation of the input does not guarantee that information extracted from the input may be accurately recalled at some later date. Certainly the effort put into type II rehearsal makes successful retrieval more likely, but as we all know, forgetting and distortions in memory do occur. In many instances, failure of recall may evidence the limited efficiency of the system; after all, the human information processing system is only human. On the other hand there are situations in which forgetting and distortions in memory have a more deliberate and purposeful role, namely those where the information is of an emotionally traumatic nature. Freud (1914) cited much clinical evidence of the individual's use of various defense mechanisms which either prevent emotionally disturbing information from being recalled, or so distort the retrieved information that its traumatic foundations are not apparent to the individual. The specific memorial processes corresponding to the Freudian defense mechanisms have yet to be determined in any detail.

The distinction between storage of information in secondary form and the nature of its subsequent retrieval is relevant to another issue associated with this locus of processing. Psychologists commonly assume that all secondary memories have previously been subject to the processes of primary memory; that is, admission to secondary memory is necessarily by way of primary memory. It is

possible, at least in theory, that this course of processing may be the "normal" means of establishing a secondary memory trace, but it is not the sole means. One of the fundamental differences between processing for primary storage and that for secondary storage is thought to be the extent of semantic analysis of the information; thus, semantic elaboration is conducive to secondary representation. Now, if preconscious semantic processing is extensive in the case of a given input, it is feasible that this information may be established as a secondary trace *without* the involvement of primary memory. This situation might occur when the "consciousness" function of primary memory is engaged with other, currently more important, inputs. Without the preliminary stage of conscious perception, however, it is likely that the only way the information might be retrieved is as a rather vague, formless mental experience or "intuition." The notion that secondary memories may be established without conscious mediation is a highly speculative one. Indeed by the very nature of the hypothesis, definitive behavioral evidence for it would be difficult to obtain. A critical test might have to await more thorough determination of neurophysiological correlates of memorial processes.

Information extracted from an input and stored in secondary memory has therefore been through a good deal of analytical and organizational processing. By way of summary it is well to acknowledge the range of extracted information that may be held in secondary form. Much of the information usually relates to the meaning of the input and its associations for the individual. Such information is said to be represented in the *semantic stratum* of secondary memory. Other strata relate to other types of extracted information.

These include representations of the input itself and of its referent. Hence the so-called *referential* stratum of secondary memory holds abstracted representations of an input's referent, either in the form of visual and verbal codes (Paivio, 1971) or in a form from which such codes may be derived (Pylyshyn, 1973). Such representation is typically quite distinct from that of the input itself: the former is of a much more abstract and generalized nature than the latter. For example, the individual's visual referential representation of the concept "tree" may not correspond precisely to any single tree the individual has seen in the past, since it is largely a generalization from such experiences. At the same time this trace can constitute the memorial referent of any given tree, or for that matter, of any written or spoken form of the word "tree." Information in the referential stratum therefore may be distinguished from the information extracted from any specific, individual input. Secondary representation of the physical or structural characteristics of a specific input itself is contained in the *structural* stratum: the form in which this information is encoded will depend upon the sensory modality of the input.

There are then three general classes of memorial information, corresponding to the semantic, referential, and structural strata of secondary memory. Of course, secondary traces are not isolated units. Links between traces exist both within strata and between strata. My memory of a tree in my garden is associated with memories of other trees (in the structural stratum), with my idealized concept of what trees look like and what they are generically called (in the referential stratum), and with my many idiosyncratic associations with trees (in semantic memory). Sets of linked traces are termed *networks*. It should not be assumed that in any given instance information extracted for secondary storage will necessarily relate to all strata. The types of information thus stored will depend very greatly on the processing requirements of the task, including the individual's expectations as to what he may subsequently have cause to recall.

Response Processes

The sensory input having been semantically processed, the information thereby derived may be given access to response processing mechanisms. Typically response processing would follow conscious perception of the information. In the case of certain simple and highly practiced responses, however, consciousness is apparently not a necessary prerequisite for response processing (Kahneman, 1973, p. 70).

Theios (1975) distinguishes two phases of response processing that precede execution of the response itself. The first of these is *response determination,* that is, the procedure of determining the cognitive response appropriate for the given input. This stage of processing may constitute a major component of the total time required for performance. Consider, for example, a situation in which the individual is presented with a printed word. If the task is to read the stimulus word, the demands of response determination would be relatively minor. On the other hand, such demands would be somewhat higher if the individual was required to classify the word according to its part of speech or some more complex dimension. In general, response determination is affected by such factors as the individual's past experience with the given combination of input and response, and the cognitive complexity of the transformation from input information to response information.

After the cognitive response has been determined, it may be appropriate to select and execute a motor response. For example, the cognitive response may be "noun," but the individual may be required to place a tick in a particular place on a form, or to give some vocal response. Theios (1975, p. 433) refers to this as *response program selection*. This stage of response processing concerns determination of the sequence of individual motor acts involved in the intended response. The efficiency of response program selection is principally a function of the commonness of the particular response.

Even in the actual execution of the motor response the system has processing demands placed upon it. Throughout performance of the response, sensory information is employed to ensure the performance is fluent and efficient. Such use of sensory information is termed feedback. For example, in making a manual response, visual information about the relative positions of hand and response instrument can be employed within a quarter of a second to modify the response sequence. Other sources of sensory feedback include kinesthetic and somasthetic stimuli. Feedback plays an essential role in response execution, for the following reason. The motor program merely defines the gross sequence of movements necessary for performance of the response; its specification is not sufficiently precise to include the fine, coordinated movements that are involved in dexterous response execution. It is in the latter regard that feedback makes its basic contribution.

Of course responses are not always correct. Usually errors in performance on a task decline with practice. In some tasks, how-

ever, errors tend to persist for some time. One general class of such
tasks is the so-called paced tasks, in which the individual has to
make a response as quickly as possible. There seems to be a link between accuracy and rate of performance in such tasks, with improved accuracy requiring a sacrifice in the speed of response execution. This is termed a speed-accuracy tradeoff, and may involve effects not merely upon response execution but also upon processes at
the levels of response determination and response program selection.

This chapter describes the processing characteristics of the
components of the human information processing system. These
characteristics are illustrated by considering the course of processing
of a sensory input for which the individual has no particular expectation. As a pedagogic device this approach adequately serves its purpose. However, it would be erroneous to suppose that the operations of the information processing system are thereby completely
specified. In the first place, we often have expectations as to what
stimuli we are about to encounter in the environment. Secondly, not
all information processed by the system comes from the environment: much of our cognitive experience is internally generated as
thoughts and images. It is possible that the nature of processing in
such situations differs fundamentally from one with sensory input.

Further, it is insufficient to characterize the information processing system simply as a set of components. The system must also
be examined as a whole, and the principles of its holistic operation
considered. These are among the issues to be taken up in the following chapter.

Chapter 3

FURTHER PROCESSING
FUNCTIONS OF THE SYSTEM

Having described the processing characteristics of each of the components of the information processing system, it is appropriate now to examine some specific modes in which the system may function. Coverage of these different processing functions must necessarily be selective, and in this chapter four particular aspects of processing are reviewed. These are, in turn, the effects of expectations on processing; individual differences in processing style; the nature of thought processes; and the mechanisms of attention.

Expectations and Information Flow

At this point the reader may have the impression that the flow of information through the processing system is always in one direction, from lower to higher levels of processing.

There is reason to believe that this is not invariably the case. Indeed one instance of information flow in the opposite direction was mentioned in the previous chapter. This concerned visual coding of an abstracted referent which is associated with the given input. Hence, for example, when the stimulus word APPLE has been encoded and semantically analyzed, there may be a downward flow of information from the level of semantic analysis to that of visual encoding, thereby establishing a visuospatial representation of an apple at the encoding locus. Under certain circumstances this visual code of the referent may be given access to primary memory and thus to consciousness, and the individual may experience a visual *image* of an apple when presented with the input APPLE. In the present context it is not the nature of mental imagery that is of major interest, but rather the fact that information can flow from higher to lower levels of processing.

Norman (1976) has explored the concept of "top-down" information flow as an explanation of the effects of expectations and context on perception of sensory inputs. We have all had the experience of misreading a particular word in a novel when we had expected to see a similar word at that point. It might not be so well appreciated, however, that we make similar use of context in (veridical) reading of prose, or for that matter, in many other perceptual tasks. Thus in reading a book we do not need to process every letter of every word. The processing system can make use of our past experience of syntactic and semantic properties of prose to form expectations about the words next to be processed. If the expectations are correct, only a very gross and incomplete analysis of the input is necessary for its pattern recognition: the general shape and length of a word, and perhaps a few letters at the beginning and end of the word, may provide sufficient information for the expectation to be confirmed and for "recognition" to occur.

Clearly such expectations are formed at a higher locus of processing than pattern recognition. In Norman's view the information representing these expectations flows down through the system and influences processes at the lower level of pattern recognition. It is likely,

therefore, that processing of sensory inputs does not invariably proceed by way of information flow from lower to higher levels. Indeed it
may be typical for this type of bottom-up processing and the contextual, top-down mode to operate conjointly, with one predominating
over the other according to the novelty of the perceptual situation.

Individual Differences in Processing Style

It was argued in Chapter 2 that human information processing is
not a matter of flow of information along rigidly defined channels.
Rather, the operation of cognitive control processes introduces a good
deal of flexibility into the processing system. In this light it is hardly
surprising to find differences among individuals in the mode of processing employed in any given cognitive task. At the same time, despite
the potential flexibility in the individual's mode of processing, it is
invariably the case that the individual has preferred or habitual styles
of information processing. Such preferred modes of processing, termed
cognitive styles, tend to be adopted over a wide range of cognitive
tasks, that is, they are to a large degree independent of the nature of
the input. It is to illustrations of a few of these that we now turn.

The most widely known and researched example of cognitive style
is the field dependence dimension. By means of a great variety of
perceptual and cognitive tests, Witkin and his associates (Witkin,
Lewis, Hertzman, Machover, Meissner, and Wapner, 1954) observed
individual differences in the extent to which subjects could isolate and
act upon a particular piece of information which is embedded in a
stimulus array. One type of task that illustrates such individual differences is the so-called "rod and frame" test. In this task the subject is

required to adjust the position of a rod until he judges it to be vertical. The rod is positioned in the center of a rectangular frame which the experimenter independently sets at an angle to the vertical. The rod and frame are illuminated, and the subject sits in an otherwise darkened room while performing the task. It is found that with some people the adjustment of the rod is markedly affected by the orientation of the surrounding frame; in contrast other subjects make their judgments of the rod's verticality quite independently of the slope of the frame. In this and other tests subjects consistently differ in their use of information from the whole perceptual field in a processing task.

Subsequent research (Witkin, Dyk, Faterson, Goodenough, and Karp, 1962) indicates that the dimension of field dependence (or field independence) is one facet of a more general type of cognitive style. At one extreme there are people who habitually adopt an *analytic* mode of processing: this is characterized by a high degree of differentiation among the informational components of the environmental stimulus array, with consequently greater cognitive complexity and dimensionality in relating pieces of information. At the other extreme individuals exhibit a *global* mode of processing, that is, one in which the stimulus array tends to be treated holistically, with relatively little articulation of constituent informational details. It is likely that these distinct styles of processing are initially effected by cognitive control processes in that region of the information processing system associated with perceptual organization and pattern recognition. More precise determination of the loci involved awaits further research.

At the same time some particularly important progress has been made in relating this dimension of cognitive style to the type of perceptual defenses employed by the individual in dealing with conflict-arousing information (Witkin, 1965). It has been found that people with an analytic processing style tend to have a relatively developed defensive structure and to use specialized, comparatively complex defense mechanisms. For example, these individuals commonly intellectualize and rationalize conflict-arousing information, thereby separating the denotative features of input from its more disturbing connotative features. Thus the analytic style of separating perceptual elements is also reflected in the individual's system of defenses. In contrast, people who adopt a global mode of processing employ comparatively gross defensive processes: hence they may completely repress conflict-arousing information, allowing neither denotative nor connotative features to intrude into consciousness. Again the global cognitive style of treating information holistically is extended to the individual's defensive structure.

People may also differ in the depth to which information is encoded and semantically elaborated before a response to it is initiated. On this basis Kagan (1966) has distinguished a *reflective* cognitive style from an *impulsive* mode. Behaviorally the distinction between these cognitive styles is most generally evidenced as a difference in conceptual tempo in making decisions.

One other major dimension of cognitive style relates to the individual's relative utilization of visual and verbal codes in mediating semantic analysis of sensory inputs and in mediation of thought processes. On the one hand there are people classified as *visualizers* who typically experience vivid visual imagery, are conscious of quasi-pictorial representations during their thinking, and report being relatively dependent upon imaginal mediation in cognitive processing. *Verbalizers*, on the other hand, report much less awareness of and use of visual images in their thinking, and appear to employ verbal representation of information across a variety of cognitive tasks. Indeed some extreme verbalizers are quite at a loss in trying to comprehend how anyone could seriously report experiencing "pictures in his head." To a strong visualizer, of course, inability to have such an experience is tantamount to total lack of imagination. More typically, however, this dimension of cognitive style reflects relative preferences between visual and verbal codes rather than total inability to utilize the non-preferred code. Hence, for example, given the particular pattern of preference in a specific individual, actual use of the codes is still sufficiently flexible that it can be varied in accordance with the processing requirements of the current situation.

A number of behavioral and physiological indexes have been found to correlate consistently with subjects' reported mode of mediation, considerably strengthening the evidential basis of the visualizer-verbalizer dimension of cognitive style (see, e.g., Paivio, 1971; Richardson, 1977). Additionally this dimension is emerging in psychological research as a significant determinant of individual differences in learning, perception, and other cognitive skills.

The dimensions of global-analytic, reflective-impulsive, and visualizer-verbalizer are but a few of the varieties of cognitive style proposed in the literature (see, e.g., Warr, 1970). Nevertheless it should be apparent even from this cursory review that the concept of cognitive style extends beyond the traditional confines of cognition, and in particular is closely associated with those aspects of behavior we refer to as personality. The information-processing approach to personality has certainly attracted some attention (see Schroder and Suedfeld, 1971). However, as yet it is not clear that such complex aspects of personality as interpersonal relations, psychosis, or ideology, for example, may be satisfactorily reduced to different habits in information processing.

For present purposes it is sufficient to record that individual differences in various cognitive aspects of behavior can be accommodated within an information processing framework. In this regard it is also noteworthy that Hunt (e.g., Hunt, Lunneborg, and Lewis, 1975) has had considerable success in elucidating the nature of individual differences in intelligence by relating them empirically to differences in processing characteristics of various loci of the system. The incorporation of individual differences into the model of the human information processing system will constitute a significant increase in the model's ecological validity.

Thought Processes

In the preceding discussions of the nature of human information processing, our concern has been almost exclusively with the means by which the system deals with inputs from the environment. Attention must now be given to cognitive processing of information that has its origins within the system itself. In other words how are the processes of *thinking* or ideation accommodated in the model of information processing? The term "thought processes" is here interpreted in a broad sense to include such diverse mental experiences as imagery, reminiscence, dreams, and problem solving.

It is immediately evident that ideation relies heavily upon information stored in (secondary) memory, and hence thought processes must involve, at least in part, retrieval of information from this store.

Thought processes may utilize information from any of the strata of secondary memory. Semantic memory would be essential for retrieval of factual information and for the elaboration of associations that is so characteristic of much of our thinking. Similarly the encoded information of the referential and structural strata of memory may play an important role as the fundamental informational source of imaginal experiences.

At the same time thought processes must involve more than mere retrieval from secondary memory. In the first place thinking, particularly problem solving, can provide new insights of which the individual was previously ignorant. Thought processes therefore may entail reorganization of information in memory as well as its retrieval. Further, ideation is much more creative and dynamic than mere location of information in memory would admit. Consider, for example, the fact that many people can visualize in their "mind's eye" such things as a purple lemon, or a horse spinning in the air, despite never having witnessed such things in real life. A model of thinking must account for this feature of *manipulation* of information retrieved from memory.

These considerations suggest that while information from various strata of secondary memory may constitute the source material for thought, there are additional processes which are applied to this information. The most probable course of processing is that the memorial information is first subjected to the processes of pattern recognition, after which the extracted information proceeds up through the system in essentially the same manner as is the case with sensory inputs. The involvement of pattern recognition processes would account for the manipulation of memorial information that is a feature of imaginal thought processes, since such manipulation also occurs with sensory inputs. For example, we can still read a word that is printed upside down: indeed pattern recognition mechanisms not only achieve recognition of the word but also encode the information that the stimulus is inverted. Similar processes may underlie an imaginal experience of, say, a horse spinning in the air.

Consistent with this model, other aspects of thought processes seem to implicate various preconscious processing loci. Thus, to the extent that the individual relies on verbal mediation in analytical thought, the formation of a verbal code at the locus of input encoding would play a fundamental role in this mode of thinking. In fact, just as the individual adopts habitual strategies for processing sensory inputs, so too are thought processes characterized by cognitive styles. For example, there is much in common between the global mode of input processing and characteristics of prelogical, intuitive thinking.

It may also be acknowledged that the proposed involvement of preconscious levels of processing in ideation can account for the fact that thought processes may proceed outside the individual's awareness. For instance, someone who has worked unsuccessfully on a problem for some time will commonly find that if he puts the problem temporarily "out of mind," a solution may subsequently "pop into his head," often at a time when he appeared to be engaged in totally unrelated activities. Perhaps also intuitive thought entails, at least in part, steps in the chain of reasoning which do not proceed beyond preconscious processing levels.

There is experimental evidence for the view that thought processes do in fact use some of the same processing mechanisms as does perception of environmental stimuli, provided cognizance is taken of sensory modality. For example, Segal and Fusella (1970) report that visual imagery interferes with the detection of visual signals, and it does so to a much greater degree than it affects detection of auditory signals. In other words, interference can occur between processing of sensory inputs and that of internally-generated information. The observation of Segal and Fusella clearly indicates the dependence of the two processing modes on some of the same processing loci. Nevertheless it remains to be shown that levels of processing below that of pattern recognition are *not* involved in the processes of thinking. Admittedly there are logical arguments against the involvement of such lower loci as the afferent stores in thought processes. The function of such storage, it will be recalled, is to hold afferent information for a period sufficient to permit further processing. This function would seem to be unnecessary in the case of thinking, since the source of information lies in secondary memory and, unlike much environmental information, is available virtually for any required period of time. Additionally it would appear that in general, variables known to affect afferent storage (without also independently affecting subsequent levels of processing) do not differentially affect thought processes. For example, the degree to which the eye is adapted to the dark has a particularly marked effect on iconic storage (Sperling, 1960), but there is no evidence that this factor has any direct bearing on the execution of visual imagery.

There is a reasonable case, then, for the account of thought processes outlined above. Under this account, such processes are held to be initiated in retrieval of information from memory. This information is admitted to the locus of pattern recognition, whence it may be mediated into consciousness by the processes of input encoding and semantic analysis.

The model of the human information processing system therefore can account both for ideation and for processing of sensory inputs. It is proposed that processing of internally-generated information and that of sensory information make demands on a number of the same processing mechanisms. The principal distinctions between the two modes of functioning lie firstly in the origins of the information, and secondly in the proposition that thought processes do not involve levels of processing below that of pattern recognition.

It may be noted in passing that one type of internally generated mental experience, namely a hallucination, may in fact depend upon some of the afferent stages of processing preceding pattern recognition. In hallucinations the individual has the impression that the informational source of the experience is in the environment rather than in his own mind. This may indicate involvement of certain afferent processes and/or afferent storage (see Barber, 1971). In this regard hallucinations might be interpreted to be an exception to the rule that thought processes call only upon loci at or above pattern recognition. At the same time it is not clear that hallucinations are purely a product of ideation: there often seems to be some element of sensory processing present in the experience.

Attention

The sensory environment of each individual comprises a great amount and variety of information to which the individual is potentially exposed. However, not all stimuli are relevant to behavior at any given moment. *Selective attention* refers to the process whereby currently irrelevant information is ignored by the individual in favor of informa-

tion which at that moment is critical to the individual's present behavior and plans for future action. Thus selective attention is held to
entail differential treatment of available sources of information according to their current relevance.

The phenomenological effects of selective attention would be
familiar to everyone. By way of illustration, consider the experience of
attending to one face in a crowd. This seems to produce a type of
"tunnel vision," a narrowed field of focus within which the attended
face appears more vivid, intense, and clear. On the other hand the
viewer's impression of unattended members of the crowd seems markedly deficient in these qualities.

This example suggests that while attended sensory information is
extensively analyzed in the individual's processing system, such may
not necessarily be the case for unattended information. The example thereby introduces an important issue in the study of attention,
namely the extent to which processing of unattended information is
restricted in order to reduce possible interference with concurrent
processing of attended information. An understanding of the nature of
selective attention rests upon an appreciation of *processing interaction*
between attended and unattended inputs: such interaction reflects the
progress of attended and unattended information through the processing system and the effects of selective control processes upon this flow.

Two types of processing interaction have been identified. One is
known as *capacity interference*, and its role in attentional phenomena
has been promoted primarily by Kahneman (1973). According to
Kahneman, the processes at many levels of the system require "effort"
or processing capacity for their operation. However, the common pool
of capacity upon which each of these processes calls is a limited re-

source, and each process must compete for capacity. It must be emphasized that these capacity resources are undifferentiated: if analysis of one input is proceeding at a particular locus, there is limited capacity available for simultaneous processing of another input at *any* level of the system. Thus while parallel processing of concurrent inputs is possible, the speed and effectiveness of such processing is typically poor, that is, capacity interference occurs.

In terms of the concept of capacity interference, then, selective attention simply involves assigning priority to the attended input in the allocation of processing capacity. Such allocation is presumably achieved by a control process in accordance with the comparative relevance of the concurrent inputs. In other words there is a "capacity allocation policy" which governs information flow at any given moment. To a large extent this prevents unattended input from interfering with processing of attended information. However, even when the capacity required for processing attended information is substantial, there is invariably some spare capacity available and this is continuously allocated to processing of other concurrent inputs. By permitting some processing of unattended inputs, such allocation has two notable effects. First, it maintains some degree of environmental monitoring: when another source of important information suddenly appears in the environment it may consequently be recognized as such at preconscious levels of processing and attention can be redirected appropriately.

Second, since there is parallel processing of attended and unattended inputs at least at some levels of the system, another type of processing interaction can occur. This is termed *structural interaction*, and involves interaction between inputs when these simultaneously occupy the *same* processing locus. Structural interaction is not simply a matter of a number of inputs competing for the same processing mechanisms: the latter is more in the nature of capacity interference. The critical factor underlying structural interaction is that at the locus concerned, the coexistence of attended and unattended information necessitates a (control) decision as to which input is the attended one—that is, which input should be given priority in capacity allocation at the next level of processing. Consistent with this view is the finding that at a variety of processing loci the discriminability of attended and unattended information is a fundamental determinant of performance in an attentional task (Irwin, 1976, 1978b). As a limited illustration of this point, suppose that you are at a noisy cocktail party and are surrounded by many small groups of people each engaged in animated conversation. Usually you will find it easier to attend to one particular conversation when other groups are discussing different topics than when everyone is talking about the same subject.

Essentially then, attention among sensory inputs reflects two distinct characteristics of the human information processing system, namely capacity interference and structural interaction. An additional selective process that is basic to attention is the choice of information that is to be admitted to consciousness. There is experimental evidence that unattended information may be excluded from primary memory (Davis and Smith, 1972). In part this may be due to the fact that unattended inputs often are not allocated sufficient processing capacity for them to reach such a high level of the system. On the other hand, provided that the capacity required for processing attended information is not too great, unattended inputs can be processed to the level of semantic analysis (see, e.g., Mackay, 1973). Under such circumstances the semantically encoded information extracted from the attended input must be discriminated from that extracted from the unattended input, and the former selected for admission to consciousness. The selective control process involved here may reasonably be deemed to fulfil an attentional function.

One further attentional phenomenon should be mentioned, and that is the relationship between attention and practice. A highly practiced task requires relatively little attention. With experience you can execute a forehand stroke in tennis with little (conscious) consideration of the position of your feet, your grip on the racket, or the position of the head of the racket throughout the swing. Practice may have two general effects on the attentional characteristics of a task. There will normally be a reduction in processing capacity allocated to the task; that is, by becoming "automatic" the practiced task requires much less mental effort. Further, practice may improve discrimination of task-relevant information from irrelevant information, thereby reducing structural interference. These changes in a task's processing characteristics that result from practice are critical to an understanding of the development of cognitive skills.

The preceding analysis of attention has been formulated in terms of selection among sensory inputs, and indeed most of the research effort in this area has been along the same lines. It must be acknowledged, however, that attentional considerations also apply to thought processes. As argued previously, these processes use a number of loci of the processing system, and therefore they will require allocation of processing capacity. In this regard, then, selection must also be made between sensory input and internally-generated information. In a sense this may be a matter of selection more between two modes of cognitive functioning than between different items of information to be processed. We attend either to our mental activities or to the external environment, and institute appropriate processing programs accordingly. Nevertheless, even while we are engrossed in our thoughts a degree of environmental monitoring is maintained. It is for this reason that, for example, someone calling your name will quickly put an end to a daydream. In that thought processes are in fact accompanied by some processing of sensory inputs, the concepts of capacity allocation and structural interaction are cogent in this situation also. The above analysis of attentional phenomena should therefore be regarded as of some generality, and not one applicable only to processing of sensory inputs.

A discussion of attention is justifiably incorporated into this chapter because attention is a significant cognitive function. In the present context, however, it also serves as a vehicle for introducing some of the more global characteristics of the human information processing system. An awareness of such concepts as processing capacity and structural interaction is indispensable to an appreciation of the model precisely because they do represent global characteristics. Their existence reminds us that we are not dealing with a series of independent processing components in which the principles of operation of any one component are completely unrelated to those of the rest of the series. On the contrary, the model does indeed represent a *system* of processing loci. Certainly within this system each locus features its own distinctive processing characteristics, because it has a specific function to perform. At the same time the function of the individual locus is no more than a sub-goal in a broader plan effected by the set of loci as a whole, and it is here that holistic principles of information processing have their foundation. The systemic character of the model is arguably its most fundamental attribute and it is essential that particular cognizance be taken of this feature.

This completes the exposition of the model of the human information processing system. It is appropriate at this point to reiterate the fact that this type of model has proved to be a valuable guide to psychologists in their attempts to understand cognitive aspects of human behavior (see, e.g., Haber, 1974; Simon, 1979). Thus the significant progress in elucidating the processing characteristics of the system has provided the foundation for modern approaches to such phenomena as attention, memory, intelligence, problem solving, and language. It may be germane, therefore, to investigate the applicability of the information processing approach to paracognitive phenomena in the hope of gaining some greater insight into their nature. Additionally the incorporation of paranormal phenomena into such a framework might encourage psychologists to expand their present conceptions of information processing. Potentially, then, consideration of paracognitive effects in information processing terms might achieve both advancement of our understanding and fruitful cross-fertilization between the fields of cognitive psychology and parapsychology.

Chapter 4

PARALLELS BETWEEN
NORMAL AND PARANORMAL COGNITION

As a preliminary to assessing the applicability of an information processing approach to paranormal cognition or *psi processing*, we shall consider some general parallels between normal and paranormal cognition. At this point there is no attempt to establish evidence of the involvement of any specific processing loci in paranormal cognition: such material is more appropriately raised in the context of selection among potential models of psi processing. It is the objective of the present chapter to determine whether or not there are sufficient general similarities between normal and paranormal cognition as to constitute a prima facie case for more detailed examination of psi phenomena in information processing terms.

Paranormal cognition is here defined as those processes underlying the cognitive characteristics of extrasensory perception. There is also a case for regarding psychokinesis (PK) as a type of paranormal cognition: however, for convenience of exposition psychokinesis is considered in a separate chapter. Thus this preliminary analysis of paranormal cognition is devoted exclusively to extrasensory perception (ESP).

In ESP the individual apparently acquires noninferential knowledge by means that do not involve any of the known senses. In this respect there would seem to be a fundamental distinction between sensory and extrasensory perception. However, the position may not be as simple as that. It is conceivable, for example, that at some future time scientists will discover a form of physical energy which is responsible for the transmission of information we currently regard as extrasensory, and that the anatomical structures sensitive to this form of energy will also be determined. People who regard ESP as a "sixth sense" would seem to assume, at least implicitly, that such discoveries will be made. Nevertheless this does not pose a problem of any significance for the information processing approach. Such an approach can only hope to account for the *processing* of extrasensorily acquired information: it is not relevant to an explanation of the means by which such information is transmitted spatially and temporally. Thus parapsychologists have yet to determine that a type of energy exists which is responsible for psi transmission, but this fact does not in itself constitute an objection to potential development of an information processing model of ESP.

Nevertheless there is an associated point that has terminological implications. In subsequent discussion of the processing characteristics of ESP the term "psi input" will be employed in connection with information acquired by extrasensory means. Some caution must be exercised in interpretation of this term, for the reason that there is no conclusive evidence that the process responsible for the acquisition of information in ESP is in fact a transmissive one at all. Therefore information may not be acquired here in the manner that the term "input" could be interpreted to suggest. Perhaps, as Gauld (1976, p. 36) argues, such information simply "happens"; ESP may be more akin to anomalous knowledge than to informational input. At the same time it is still legitimate to inquire into the means by which the individual becomes conscious of such "anomalous knowledge," and to explore this question within an information processing framework. The term "psi input" will be employed in this context to refer to that information in the processing system which is the source of the experience of ESP. Hence psi input is defined to be *within* the system, and should not be regarded as an environmental stimulus. It may prove to have its origins in such a stimulus, or it may just "happen" in the system, but in no way should the use of the term *psi input* be taken in itself as an assumption of the former view in preference to the latter. The term psi source is employed in a similar, noncommittal way to designate the object or event in the environment to which the psi experience is presumed to be related.

A basic issue in psi processing, then, is the manner in which psi input reaches the level of consciousness and, in the present context, whether this features similarities to processes of normal cognition. One fairly gross level of comparison concerns the form of the experience. Various forms of ESP experience have been reported: they include visual images or "visions," dreams, hallucinations (in any sensory modality), and nonvisual intuitive experiences or "impressions." Since these experiences are also found in situations not regarded as paranormal, there is nothing at this level of classification which discourages application of an information processing approach. However, a more substantial assessment of this issue can be gleaned from comparisons between normal and paranormal cognition in more specific terms.

Extrasensory perception is a notoriously unstable and fragile phenomenon and, particularly in experimental situations, its effects are typically small in magnitude. These and other considerations suggest that psi inputs are in some sense relatively weak. It is therefore appropriate to explore the comparison between ESP and the perception of very weak sensory inputs or *subliminal perception.* Considerable research effort has been devoted to the study of perception of subliminal stimuli. In the typical experimental procedure of such studies, the subject is presented with a visual stimulus of such brief duration and/or low intensity that he reports being completely unaware of the nature of the stimulus. Nevertheless various behavioral measures indicate that at a preconscious level semantic information may in fact be extracted from the input, at least under certain conditions (Dixon, 1971). For example, this information may result in ideas coming to mind without the subject's being aware that such ideas have their informational origin in the subliminal stimulus.

Now, in comparing ESP to subliminal perception, it must be acknowledged immediately that there is little reason to believe that ESP is the product of a weak sensory stimulus. Therefore any similarities between the two phenomena might only reflect characteristics of processing *above* the level of afferent analysis. With this in mind a number of parallels may be drawn. Strong performance in both ESP and subliminal perception is facilitated by the same general state of consciousness. The nature of this conducive state will be discussed in more detail in a subsequent chapter, but it is characterized in part by an uncritical, relaxed yet alert frame of mind. There is also some evidence that performance in both tasks is improved by minimizing the amount of extraneous sensory input in the situation. This situational variable and the previously cited conducive state of consciousness would appear to relate to attentional characteristics of the two phenomena.

Additionally there are similarities between the performance

characteristics of ESP and subliminal perception. Evidence of these is found in studies of performance of a common task under two different experimental conditions. Typically, one condition entails subliminal exposure of stimuli; in another condition, stimuli are not exposed at all and information is presumed to be available by paranormal means alone. In one such study by Nash and Nash (1963), accuracy of performance fell significantly both within and across blocks of trials, under the ESP condition and under the condition of subliminal exposure. These so-called decline effects are well documented in parapsychological research (see, e.g., Rhine, 1969), and the observation of such effects in subliminal perception is therefore all the more notable. Further, Stanford's (1974c) analysis of the data from a similar study produced a significant positive correlation between performances under the two conditions: subjects who were successful with subliminally exposed stimuli also tended to score relatively highly in the ESP task. To an extent an incidental observation by Wiklund (1975) supports and extends this possible relationship. His subjects worked on a perceptual task in which the response can be biased in a particular direction by the introduction of subliminal stimuli into the situation. However, Wiklund found three subjects who consistently responded in the *opposite* direction to that normally produced by the subliminal cues. In an ESP condition of the same task, these same subjects exhibited significant *psi-missing*, that is, they selected incorrect responses much more frequently than expected by chance. This observation in a small way reinforces the view that the performance characteristics of ESP and subliminal perception are similar.

Such data are consistent with the hypothesis that ESP involves the same processing loci as subliminal perception, at least above the level of afferent processing. While the data are certainly suggestive in this regard, they may not be definitive. It is possible that performance in tasks of subliminal perception actually involves an element of psi: that is, success in such tasks is in part due to utilization of extrasensory information in the situation. To the extent that such a factor is operative it might account for similarities and correlations cited above. It should be noted, however, that there is reason to believe ESP does not contribute significantly to performance on tasks of subliminal perception. For example, Kreitler and Kreitler (1973) report evidence that the individual may selectively process either extrasensory or subliminal information, but apparently he can not further enhance performance by utilizing both sources of information simultaneously. In this light it may be maintained that the relationships between ESP and subliminal perception do encourage exploration of psi processing in information-processing terms.

There is one other parallel between these phenomena that warrants acknowledgment. In normal cognition it is typically the case that whenever the individual becomes aware of some item of semantic information, he is also aware of the source of the information: it is recognized as having its origins either in a particular, sensorily accessible part of the environment, or in the individual's own mind. In ESP, on the other hand, information enters consciousness generally without any clues as to how it got there. As far as the individual is concerned, the information was not extracted from any sensory input, nor was it a product of his imagination. In the context of normal cognition, then, ESP would appear to be anomalous in this regard. Indeed so it would be but for the fact that subliminal perception exhibits the same characteristic. Thus in both ESP and subliminal perception, concepts come to mind without concomitant information to relate them to sensory or imaginal sources. Since the "normal" cognitive phenomenon of subliminal perception has this property, it may not be necessary to invoke any paranormal principle to account for this characteristic in psi processing, and in fact it would be parsimonious not to do so.

There are therefore a number of indications that processing of a psi input is similar to that of a very weak sensory input. Consequently it may be instructive to consider another phenomenon associated with cognitive processing of weak sensory inputs, namely *perceptual defense*. Evidence from a variety of sources demonstrates that the individual can to some extent protect himself from the perception of inputs that are emotionally disturbing, conflict arousing, or otherwise disagreeable in nature. When one is attending to the source of such input and the stimulus is at least moderate in intensity, perception can not be avoided and other defensive measures of a behavioral kind must be taken. However, where the emotionally laden input is not currently being attended to, or has either low intensity or short duration, certain defensive perceptual processes may come into play. Some of these processes may be attentional, serving to keep the information out of consciousness if need be. Perceptual defensiveness may also affect processes at a number of preconscious loci. The experiment by Worthington (1964), described in Chapter 2, illustrates this point. Here, it will be recalled, subjects were relatively reluctant to report the mere presence of a very dim light when, unknown to the subjects, it comprised an emotionally charged word. Such defensive reactions may be termed *repression*, since their objective is to inhibit the entry of disagreeable information into consciousness. Another perceptual defense is *reaction formation*, in which the semantic content of the relevant input is negated. Hence the individual's reactions to subliminal stimuli may be completely contrary to his responses when the stimuli are supraliminal (Smith and Henriksson, 1955; Wiklund, 1975).

To the extent that psi processing parallels processing of a weak sensory input it is germane to inquire whether or not such defensive processes occur in ESP. It is certainly well established that the individual's attitude to ESP has a fundamental effect upon the nature of his performance in such a task (see Palmer, 1971, for a review). This may plausibly be linked to the operation of defensive processes. Research of greater evidential value has been performed by Johnson and his colleagues (e.g., Johnson, 1975; Johnson and Kanthamani, 1967). In a series of studies Johnson has found a consistent relationship between scores on ESP tasks and those on an independently developed measure of perceptual defensiveness known as the Defense Mechanism Test (DMT). Indeed using the DMT it is possible to some extent to identify certain people who tend to employ repression as a perceptual defense, and others whose method of dealing with weak sensory inputs is more akin to reaction formation. Johnson (1975; Johnson and Lübke, 1977) reports that there is some suggestive evidence that the former type of subject performs at chance levels in ESP tests, whereas the latter type exhibits psi-missing, that is, makes more incorrect responses than expected by chance. The latter effect is supported by Wiklund's (1975) observation, cited above, that three subjects who showed reaction formation in a subliminal perception task were also strong psi-missers.

Other ostensibly defensive characteristics of ESP may be noted. For example, where the extrasensory experience features visual imagery, the image is typically distorted and fragmented in relation to the

"target" or external referent of the experience. This is most clearly
demonstrated in experiments in which subjects attempt to draw pictorial or concrete targets on the basis of psi information (Ehrenwald,
1976; Puthoff and Targ, 1976; Warcollier, 1948). Ehrenwald (1975)
points out the similarity between such drawings and those of brain-
damaged patients suffering visual agnosia, and argues that in both cases
the individual has difficulty in organizing his perceptions into meaningful wholes. Similar processes of fragmentation are known to occur in
eidetic imagery (Klüver, 1930). These organizational disturbances in
ESP could well be of a defensive nature. In any event their occurrence
in situations not regarded as paranormal does point to the feasibility of
accounting for this characteristic of ESP within an information processing framework. Another defensive mechanism which can operate in
ESP is the admission of the information to consciousness in a *symbolic*
form (Rhine, 1953; Roll, 1966, p. 512). Now, symbolic representation is
a normal feature of dreams and other types of mental imagery, and thus
it should be possible to accommodate this defensive function in an
information processing approach to psi. More important, in the present
context, is the observation that very weak sensory inputs also tend to
elicit symbolic responses (Dixon, 1971, pp. 78–81).

Defensive processes in ESP therefore correspond closely to those
associated with the perception of a weak sensory stimulus. At this point
it is evident that there are indeed many parallels between processing of
psi inputs and that of weak sensory inputs. On this basis it might be
deemed appropriate to now consider the possible involvement of individual processing loci in ESP. However it must not be forgotten that in
spite of the parallels educed above, ESP does *not* stem from weak
sensory stimulation. A weak input it may in some sense be, but it is not

"sensory" within our current understanding of that term. While it is unlikely that we will overlook the latter characteristic when we attempt to model ESP in information processing terms, it is nonetheless possible that such an attempt may be biased if it is founded solely upon similarities between ESP and sensory processing. In the interests of balance it is necessary therefore to consider the possibility of similarities between psi processing and that other mode of normal cognitive functioning, namely processing of internally-generated information or *ideation*.

As noted in Chapter 3, the systemic source of thought processes is (secondary) memory. Hence in relating ESP to thought processes, a fundamental level of comparison would be that between psi processing and recall of information from memory. In fact a good deal of theoretical and empirical attention has been given to such a comparison. The theoretical issues will be discussed subsequently in relation to different models of psi processing, but it is appropriate here to sketch the background of this area of research. Prior to the mid-1960's there was some intermittent speculation on the involvement of memorial structures and processes in ESP (e.g., Marshall, 1960; Price, 1964). However, the principal impetus for research on this issue was provided by Roll (1966). In this paper Roll argued that many apparently unrelated characteristics of ESP can be integrated under the hypothesis that psi information actually consists of the percipient's own memories. Extrasensory perception, Roll held, was more akin to remembering than to perceiving. Thus certain information represented in some of the individual's memory traces is relevant to the psi source or target, and extrasensory activation of those traces may result in mediation of the relevant information into consciousness. Roll further maintained that such mediation of psi information is governed by the principles of normal cognitive processing, including the laws of association.

(What evidence is there to link ESP with processes of memory?/A number of writers have commented that good ESP subjects, mediums, or "sensitives" tend to have exceptional memories (see Roll, 1966, p. 510 for a review). Tenhaeff (1972), for example, cites many examples of sensitives with particular memory skills relevant to the qualitative nature of their psi performance. Some observations in parapsychological laboratories may also be pertinent here. Thus Johnson (1968) and Honorton (1972) report that success in ESP tests is positively correlated with frequency of dream recall. This correlation may well reflect memorial processes common to both situations. On the other hand there may be other common factors responsible for the result. For example, it is not implausible that people characterized by low defensiveness should show both good ESP and frequent dream recall.

A more direct examination of the issue was undertaken by Feather (1967). She tested a group of subjects on an ESP task using the standard ESP cards. (Each of these cards features one of the following symbols: a square, a circle, a star, wavy lines, or a plus sign.) Additionally each subject was tested for memory of a long list of the standard ESP symbols. In the latter task subjects were given a short period for memorization and were then engaged in another activity for quite some minutes before being instructed to recall the list of symbols. Performance on this task would thus reflect processes of *secondary* memory. Feather found a significant positive correlation between ESP scores and performance on the (secondary) memory task.

Relevant data are also available in the work of Kanthamani and Rao (1974). The subjects of this study were first given a brief period of time in which they tried to memorize twenty pairs of words. This was followed by some interfering activities for two to three minutes. Each subject was then presented with a response sheet attached to a sealed opaque envelope. On the response sheet there was a list of twenty words, one from each of the word pairs the subject had previously attempted to memorize. The "memory" component of the test was to try to recall the other member of each pair, writing the response in the appropriate space on the response sheet. The "ESP" component of the test was to determine, by whatever means, the member of each pair that was listed on a card inside the sealed envelope, circling each selected item on the response sheet. Across four series of tests Kanthamani and Rao consistently found that stimuli for which recall was correct tended to be associated with significant ESP; on the other hand ESP scores for incorrectly recalled word pairs did not reach statistical significance. In similar experiments by Kreiman (1975) and Kanthamani and Rao (1975) this result was extended by the additional finding of *psi-missing* in association with incorrect recall.

These studies are evidentially more valuable than Feather's (1967) correlational experiment in that they suggest extrasensory processes are not merely *similar* to those underlying performance in memory tasks, but rather ESP in some way *depends* upon memorial processes for its expression.

This view is consistent with some of the performance characteristics of ESP. For example, the operation of defensive processes in ESP might be interpreted in the context of the various defense mechanisms which Freud (1914) recognized as critical determinants of recall. Hence chance scoring might be linked with repression, and psi-missing with reaction formation. Further, the decline effect so characteristic of

ESP (Rhine, 1969) has also been observed in performance over a series
of memory tasks (Roll, 1966, p. 509). Of course this does not account
for the decline effect, but it does suggest that the effect can be explained in terms of certain processing characteristics of memory.

Another important feature of ESP is that generally the percipient
is unable to identify the source of the information either as a sensory
input or as mentally generated. Now, if psi input has its origins in
memory, why does the individual typically fail to identify the information as internally generated? The following two points may be relevant
here. In the first place, the individual may also be unaware of the
mental origins of information in normal cognitive processing. For
example, when a problem is temporarily put aside, the solution may
subsequently reveal itself, with no indication as to where the idea came
from. Secondly, awareness of the mental origin of certain information
may be contingent upon evidence that search processes (a type of
cognitive control process) were instituted to locate the information in
memory and to activiate it for retrieval. In the case of ESP it is conceivable that extrasensory activation of a memory trace is direct: that is, it
may not involve such search processes, and the systemic origin of the
information thus remains unknown.

There are reasonable indications, therefore, that it may be appropriate to model psi processing along the lines of memory retrieval. At
first blush this conclusion may appear inconsistent with the suggestion
advanced earlier, that ESP was similar to the processing of weak sensory inputs; how can ESP parallel both of these disparate modes of
cognitive functioning? It must be remembered, however, that the
comparison between the processing of psi inputs and that of weak
sensory inputs might well be meaningful only above the locus of affe-

rent processing in the information processing system. With due cognizance of this point, it may be possible to resolve this issue within an information processing framework. As maintained in the previous chapter, the processing loci responsible for mediating memorial information into consciousness are precisely those above the level of afferent processing. The various types of evidence reported in the present chapter may therefore be compatible at least at a general level of description. Such evidence might be interpreted as suggesting that in ESP, psi inputs have their origins in memory and may thence be mediated into consciousness in a manner which indicates that they are in some sense very weak inputs.

The limitations of this description must nevertheless be emphasized. It is far too general to be regarded as a "model" of ESP: any number of specific models of psi processing might well be consistent with this outline. Further, even in this general form, the description is still a tentative one. To provide it with sounder evidential foundations it is necessary to examine in more detail the involvement of particular processing loci in ESP. These and associated issues are taken up in subsequent chapters.

At the same time it must also be remembered that the objective of the above review was not the development of a model of ESP, but rather the determination of the prima facie relevance of an information processing approach to psi phenomena. In this regard the essential implication of the review is clear: there are indeed reasonable grounds for further exploration of psi processing within an information processing framework.

Chapter 5

INFORMATION PROCESSING MODELS
OF PARANORMAL COGNITION

The present stage of development of the thesis may be restated as follows. It may be worthwhile to construct an information processing model of paranormal cognition, provided that this can be based upon evidence of the involvement of specific processing loci in extrasensory perception. Before examining the availability of such evidence, however, it is pertinent to identify the types of information processing models that might be explored. Only in a context of alternative potential models is it possible to realize the significance of the involvement of particular processing loci and the noninvolvement of other loci.

The intention of this chapter is therefore to formulate in general terms some alternative information processing views of ESP. These fall into two broad categories, respectively designated "pseudosensory models" and "memory models." The nature and theoretical antecedents of each category will be discussed in turn. No attempt is made to systematically examine all manner of theories about ESP; exhaustive reviews of this type are available elsewhere (e.g., Rao, 1977). In the following analysis specific theories are employed simply to sketch the background of contrasting approaches available within an information processing framework.

Pseudosensory Models of ESP

In the lay mind ESP is commonly thought of as a "sixth sense," and indeed much of the terminology dating from the earliest days of parapsychological research tends to preserve this interpretation, at least implicitly. The theoretical encapsulation of this assumption is that while ESP apparently does not utilize any of the *known* sensory inputs, there is some as yet undiscovered organ, a "third eye," responsible for the reception of so-called extrasensory information. Under this view, psi inputs would be processed in essentially the same manner as sensory inputs.

This particular pseudosensory characterization of ESP is favored by very few professional parapsychologists today. This statement is not intended to prejudge the approach, but merely to indicate that adequately specified examples of such a model are rare. One model of clairvoyance that falls into this category has been described by Tart (1966). In terms of this model, information originating at an object or event is received by a processing mechanism that serves the function of "decoding" the information into a form which can be handled by the processing system. One of the possibilities considered by Tart (1966, p. 494) is that the decoding mechanism produces neural impulses. This is precisely the function of sensory transduction that is achieved by the sense organs. Hence this model of Tart's is essentially a pseudosensory type.

At the same time it is possible that extrasensory information originates in the system at some level of preconscious processing above the sense organs, and that from this point onwards the information is subject to the same processing program as a sensory input. For example,

psi input may have its systemic origin at the level of pattern recognition, and thence be encoded and semantically analyzed in the manner
of sensory inputs. Such a scheme would also fall into the category of
pseudosensory models. In view of the variety of preconscious processing loci at which extrasensory inputs might conceivably have their
initial effect, there would be corresponding variety in the different
pseudosensory models of ESP that could be proposed. Testing among
these models must necessarily relate to evidence of the involvement of
each such locus in psi processing.

Memory Models of ESP

Models in this category characterize psi processing as more akin to
thought processes than to perception. More specifically, they propose
that extrasensory inputs have their systemic origins in memory. A
number of theories of ESP are compatible with this notion in one form
or another.

One of the most provocative theories of this type is that of Bergson
(1914). Maintaining a dualist position, Bergson argued that memories
are stored not in the brain but in a nonmaterial mind. The brain does
not produce memory traces; rather its function is to exclude all irrelevant sensory information from the mind. Once the brain has identified
the currently most relevant source of information in the environment,
the mind perceives this part of the environment *directly*, that is, by
clairvoyant means. However, says Bergson, the brain is not perfectly
efficient in its attentional role, and hence the mind may establish both
relevant and irrelevant clairvoyant memories without the involvement

of the brain and the sense organs. It is perhaps unfair to strip Bergson's theory of its dualist orientation and to reformulate it in information processing terms. Thus Bergson simply did not regard normal memories as comprising information extracted from sensory inputs. Nevertheless his theory does incorporate the notion that in ESP, information not received by the sense organs can be acquired directly by memory. A similar approach has been explored more recently by Moncrieff (1951).

Another theoretical construct of relevance here is that of a universal or collective unconscious. It has been proposed that our minds do not exist as isolated, discrete units, but that they merge together at a subconscious level to form a type of collective mind. The so-called collective unconscious may contain the memories of all members of all species, or it may represent a "group mind" peculiar to specific groups or species (see, e.g., Hardy, 1950). This concept has been applied to the phenomenon of telepathy (e.g., Carington, 1945; Price, 1940). Thus under certain conditions the individual can become aware of information in the collective unconscious, giving the impression that the information has been "communicated" extrasensorily from one mind to another. Here, then, ESP (or at least telepathy) is held to be due to a paranormal expansion of the memories to which the individual has access. A telepathic experience entails retrieval of those paranormally acquired traces.

Another theory relating ESP to memory was proposed by Marshall (1960). According to this view memory entails the brain's resonance with a past state of itself, and telepathy is a resonance of one person's brain with that of another individual. In information processing terms, the activation of a trace in one person's memory can tend to exert a direct influence on another person's memorial processes, establishing a trace of similar "structure" in the recipient's memory.

As mentioned previously, Roll (1966) has also proposed a memory model of ESP. He argues that an external extrasensory stimulus activates the percipient's memory traces. This information may be mediated into consciousness and may affect behavior. However, these are merely subsidiary aspects of the ESP process: it is in memory that psi inputs have their initial effect (Roll, 1966, p. 507).

A more recent theory of ESP also should be mentioned, principally because it has attracted considerable attention. Stanford (1974a) has formulated what he terms a "psi-mediated instrumental response" (PMIR) model. Under this model psi is employed to monitor the environment for information which is relevant to the individual's needs. When such information is located there is a consequent facilitation of those responses related to fulfilment of the particular need. In short, ESP entails psi-mediated facilitation or elicitation of need-related responses. It should be noted that Stanford employs the term "response" in a very broad sense. He intends it to refer not only to motor activities, but also to such subjective events as thinking, reminiscence, and emotion. This theory has generated a deal of experimental research primarily related to Stanford's postulates on the nature of PMIRs and the conditions under which they may be elicited. However, the PMIR model does not address itself to the issue of the processing locus at which psi inputs have their initial expression. It is clear from Stanford's use of the term "response" that he does *not* envisage ESP as having its first point of contact with the processing system in the region we have labeled response processing mechanisms. It is indeed possible that the

PMIR model could be elaborated into a memory model, but in its present form it is more concerned with teleological issues than with systemic bases.

There are therefore many theoretical antecedents for formulating memory models of ESP in information processing terms. Although the above review of earlier theories is by no means exhaustive, it is sufficient to indicate one important factor in which memory models may differ, namely the origin of the memory trace that forms the basis of the ESP experience. On the one hand it is possible that psi is associated with the formation of a completely new trace in the percipient's memory. There are elements of this notion in the theories of Bergson and Marshall, and arguably also in the "collective unconscious" approach to ESP. On the other hand psi may merely activate a trace that already exists in the individual's memory; this is the view expounded by Roll. In this regard, therefore, two fundamentally distinct memory models of ESP may be proposed, one involving paranormal acquisition of memories and the other, paranormal activation of pre-existing memories (see also Blackmore, 1977).

An additional issue to which earlier theories gave scant attention is the type of trace involved. Is the trace composed of structural information, referential information, or semantic information, or indeed some combination of these? The stratum of memory in which the psi input is represented is thus another dimension upon which memory models may vary.

Finally, a memory model of ESP should also specify the means by which memorial information is mediated into consciousness or otherwise produces its behavioral effects. The earlier theories reviewed above are generally inadequate in this regard. Certainly identification of the systemic origins of psi input is a critical issue, but it is likely that the nature of the ESP experience itself also reflects the subsequent course of processing of this information.

In generating an information processing model of paranormal cognition we are therefore faced with a series of choices. The first choice that must be made is between pseudosensory models and memory models. Having decided on the general class of model preferred, a selection must then be made from the alternative models within this class. It has been the function of this chapter to indicate the nature of the options available at each of these points of choice.

Chapter 6

SELECTION AND DEVELOPMENT OF
A MODEL OF PARANORMAL COGNITION

Pseudosensory Models versus Memory Models

In formulating an information processing model of extrasensory perception, the first decision to be made is on the general framework of the model. Should a pseudosensory approach be adopted, or is a memory model to be preferred?

Evidence reviewed in Chapter 4 tends to favor the latter framework. The data of Kanthamani and Rao (1974) were particularly suggestive of the dependence of ESP upon memorial processes for its expression. In view of such data it is necessary to inquire if pseudosensory models have any compelling evidential support, and hence whether or not such a framework should be considered further.

A number of parallels have been drawn between ESP and subliminal perception (Chapter 4). It should be noted, however, that these do not constitute conclusive evidence for a pseudosensory model. The essential implication of such parallels is that psi inputs seem to be in some sense *weak* inputs, and this feature can be accommodated just as readily within a memory model as in a pseudosensory one.

The main source of evidence sometimes taken to support the pseudosensory approach concerns claims that there are forms of physical energy which could carry extrasensory information and which would exhibit the ostensible transmissive characteristics of ESP. Perhaps the currently most favored hypothesis of this type is that telepathy is carried by extremely low frequency (ELF) electromagnetic waves (Kogan, 1966; Persinger, 1975; Taylor, 1975). There are, however, many problems with this approach. In the first place the ELF-wave hypothesis is of limited generality. While it may be applicable to telepathy, it is not a viable account of clairvoyance (Taylor, personal communication, 1978), nor a likely basis for explaining precognition. Additionally, and perhaps more important in the present context, it is not known how ELF waves enter the central nervous system. Taylor (1975) does cite some evidence that this form of radiation can stimulate nerve cells directly. Nevertheless in the case of ESP it is not clear whether ELF waves would have their initial effect in afferent pathways, as supposed in pseudosensory models, or in some part of the brain itself. The latter possibility could well be held to be highly compatible with a memory model of ESP. This argument applies to all radiation theories of ESP and indeed to other hypotheses which conceive ESP to have a physical basis (see Rao, 1977, for a review). Until this matter is resolved evidence cited for any physical mode of extrasensory "transmission" can not be deemed necessarily to favor pseudosensory models of ESP.

Another difficulty with the pseudosensory approach concerns the processing locus of pattern recognition. Conscious perception of any type of information, be it internally generated or derived from sensory input, must depend upon pattern recognition. Unless the information has characteristics which can be matched against those we have experienced in the past, the information simply can not be perceived. Thus on logical grounds alone any model of ESP must incorporate the locus of pattern recognition. Indeed, as will be seen later, there is empirical evidence of the involvement of this locus in psi processing.

Now, under a pseudosensory model this conclusion implies that psi input must enter the information processing system either at or below the level of pattern recognition. The number of admissable models of this type is thereby immediately restricted. Additionally the nature of pattern recognition in paranormal cognition must be shown to be satisfactorily explained by the inclusion of the locus of pattern recognition in a pseudosensory framework. There are indications that this may not be the case, essentially for the following reason. Pattern recognition processes are critically dependent upon the "quality" or "sensory" discriminability of the input. Thus, for example, such factors as contrast, and size, form, and orientation of the stimulus object affect the efficiency of pattern recognition. Under a pseudosensory model of ESP which incorporates this locus of processing, performance in an ESP task therefore should vary systematically with target discriminability. However, in surveys of the literature by Rao (1966, pp. 71–73) and by Pratt, Rhine, Smith, Stuart, and Greenwood (1940, Ch. 13) it was found that such factors either had no effect on performance, or had an effect interpretable as a function of the subject's psychological reactions (e.g., attitudes and expectancies) to these factors rather than as a function of discriminability itself. Admittedly there is a slight possibility that to date parapsychologists have been looking at inappropriate dimensions of target discriminability. Even so, under any pseudosensory model which assumes a physical mode of ESP "transmission," it is difficult to explain why a change in the size of the target does not affect scores in a task of clairvoyance (Pratt and Woodruff, 1939).

On the other hand such results can be readily accommodated if it is assumed that in ESP, pattern recognition applies not to the primitive features of the target but to the features encoded in memory traces that are relevant to the target. Of course, only in memory models of paranormal cognition is it proposed that the input subject to pattern recognition comprises memorial features rather than features of an environmental stimulus.

While it has not been shown conclusively that pseudosensory models should be dismissed, it is apparent that they remain a theoretical option lacking in evidential foundations. By contrast, memory models certainly enjoy general empirical support (as was demonstrated in Chapter 4). In the present state of knowledge, therefore, it seems at the very least more parsimonious to adopt a memory model of ESP than one of a pseudosensory type. It is upon these grounds that we now proceed to consider the alternatives within a "memory" framework.

Selection of a Memory Model

It will be recalled that one factor differentiating among memory models of paranormal cognition relates to the origin of the memory trace underlying the ESP experience. Do psi inputs serve to estab-

lish an entirely new memory trace, or do they simply activate a
pre-existing trace?

An essential characteristic of ESP is that the individual acquires
information of which he was previously unaware. In view of this it
might be concluded that psi has created a new memory trace rather
than arousing an old one. However, this may not necessarily be the
case. It is possible, for example, that the newly acquired information
corresponds to the collective activation of a number of established
traces. An illustration should prove instructive at this point. Suppose
that by extrasensory means you learn of the death of your friend
John in a car accident some distance away. Now, to your knowledge
John has never died before, so there can not have been a (single)
trace in your memory corresponding to John's death in his car.
However, this is too simplistic a view of memory. Even after confirmation of John's death there will not be an individual trace in
your memory corresponding to this event. Rather there will be a
network of traces, linking "John," "car," "death," and other information. The extrasensory experience can therefore be explained as an
activation of a number of traces that correspond to the elements of
this network. The significant point is that each discrete piece of information is already contained in memory at the time of the experience: there is stored information about John, about death, and so
on.

Of course, if extrasensory activation of a set of memory traces is
followed by conscious perception of the corresponding objects or
events, the information may be further processed in the usual manner to enable its representation in (secondary) memory as a more

durable trace-network. For the initial experience itself, however, it can be argued that only the component elements of the network need be present in memory: the associative links between these elements need not exist. In theory this approach can be extended to account for extrasensory perception of objects, places, people, or concepts not previously encountered.

It is therefore feasible that ESP results from activation of established traces rather than from the formation of new ones. This view is consistent with much empirical evidence. Roll (1966) cites a variety of cases of spontaneous ESP which suggest paranormal activation of pre-existing memories. Many experimental investigations also have demonstrated that information held in secondary memory may subsequently be used as the vehicle for "retrieving" psi inputs; some of this evidence was reviewed in Chapter 4.

Nevertheless, while it is clear that paranormal cognition *can* involve established memory traces, it can not be shown that it must always do so. In this respect, then, there is no conclusive evidence against the alternative hypothesis that the informational source of the ESP experience is a new, paranormally produced memory trace. Once more we are in the position of having to select what seems to be, in the present state of knowledge, the most viable approach among the available options. Accordingly the memory model of ESP outlined below incorporates Roll's (1966) postulate of paranormal activation of *established* memory traces.

A second issue for decision in formulating a memory model is the stratum (or strata) of memory which contains the psi-activated traces. Secondary memory, it will be recalled, stores information at different levels of representation. In the semantic stratum are stored all the associational links between items that the individual has derived from personal experience. Abstracted representations of referents of inputs, in the form of visual and verbal codes, are held in the so-called referential stratum. Additionally the physical or structural characteristics of particular inputs themselves (as distinct from referents) may be represented in the structural stratum of secondary memory. Now, suppose the printed word TABLE is the target in an ESP task and that this target is associated with paranormal activation of a memory trace in the percipient's information processing system. Does the systemic source of the consequent ESP experience comprise the meaning of this stimulus, defined in terms of a range of the percipient's personal experiences with tables in the past? Or is the systemic source an encoded visual representation of a table, or an encoded representation of the name of this word, in the referential stratum of memory? Or is there psi-activation of a structural trace corresponding to a visual representation of the word TABLE itself? Or may any one or more of these strata be activated, depending on the particular situation?

A good deal of evidence suggests that the structural stratum may be critically involved in ESP. Perhaps this is most clearly demonstrated in studies employing pictures as targets. Sinclair (1962) reports one occasion when, acting as the agent in a telepathic task, he made a line drawing of a volcano featuring a cone and clouds of dark smoke. The percipient, Sinclair's wife, responded with an excellent representation of the target figure, but she was unable to identify the figure and hazarded a guess that it looked like a black beetle.

This is consistent with the view that, at least in this particular case, traces in the structural stratum of memory had been activated. Further, there was apparently no such activation in the referential stratum of either the name "volcano" or any abstracted visual representation of what Mrs. Sinclair thought to characterize a volcano. Similarly, traces in the semantic stratum, representing the concept of a volcano and its associations, do not appear to have been involved.

Of course the remarkable veridicality of Mrs. Sinclair's drawing of the volcano is not typical of studies in which less gifted subjects have attempted to draw pictorial or concrete targets purely on the basis of psi. In such experiments percipients' drawings are commonly observed to be distorted, fragmented, and disorganized in relation to the target. Even here, however, the data are consistent with the view that structural traces of memory are paranormally activated. The essence of the supportive evidence in these studies is that the distortions in the subjects' drawings are largely structural in nature (cf. Ehrenwald, 1976; Puthoff and Targ, 1976, p. 346; Warcollier, 1948). Thus the distortions do not tend to stem from the target object's name or functions, for example. The origins of these effects are not at issue here. The important point is that they do represent distortions of structural information, suggesting that the systemic source of the psi experience entails data on the structural features of the target.

It is notable that these effects are not peculiar to experimental studies with pictorial targets. Similar types of distortion are also found in spontaneous cases of intuitive ESP (Rhine, 1962). On the

other hand it is not yet clear if the tendency of errors in ESP performance to be structural may be generalized to any type of target.
There is a dearth of laboratory investigations in which nonvisual
targets are employed. For example, we do not know if extrasensory
perception of a purely auditory stimulus (clairaudience) is subject to
structural distortions of acoustic and articulatory features. A technical difficulty here is that in many instances structural distortions are
very subtle and can be established only through application of special statistical techniques (see Thalbourne, 1978).

Nevertheless there is adequate evidence to implicate the structural stratum of memory in paranormal cognition. This does not
demonstrate, of course, that traces in other strata are not the systemic source of ESP (see Chari, 1967; Delin, 1977). It is therefore
pertinent to inquire if there are any data which suggest, for example, that semantic traces may be paranormally activated without any
structural correlates. Well, there are cases of spontaneous ESP in
which the individual's experience is purely emotional. There may be
an acute feeling of grief with no attendant information on the cause
for such a reaction; frequently the percipient will then proceed to
rationalize the experience and conclude that a close friend or relative has died. Similarly the paranormal experience may be a purely
motor one. The individual may suddenly feel immobilized, or
pushed to one side by an unseen force; again a rationale for the experience must be deduced subsequently.

In these experiences, awareness of structural information is lacking. On the other hand, such experiences are relatively uncommon
among cases of spontaneous ESP (Rhine, 1962), suggesting that they

may be modifications of a more typical process. Indeed it is possible that experiences in which the percipient is unaware of structural information nevertheless have their systemic origin in the structural stratum of memory. The reason for this is that structural information must be further processed before having any identifiable effect on the percipient. In the case of purely motor reactions, this information may remain at a preconscious level and serve to mediate the motor response without entering consciousness. Similarly, in the purely emotional ESP experience, structural information may be processed but only the connotative semantic code admitted to primary memory and consciousness. Such "structureless" experiences show a certain similarity to subliminal perception, in which structural information is extracted but does not reach consciousness. The involvement of mediational processes may also account for those cases of ESP in which there seem to be *conceptual* distortions, as in dreams for example. These may be accommodated under the structural activation hypothesis if it is assumed that such distortions arise not from the systemic source of the information but from the operation of defensive processes at the locus of semantic analysis.

In the memory model to be formulated below, it is proposed that in ESP, memory traces are activated at the structural level of secondary memory. As we have seen, this postulate is consistent with much of the available data, and other ostensibly inconsistent data can be accommodated if it is assumed that mediation of structural information from memory follows that of normal cognition. The basis of the latter assumption can be fully appreciated only when we examine the involvement of specific processing loci in extrasensory processing.

ESP and Specific Processing Loci

At this point in the development of a model of ESP, a preference has been established for a model in which established traces in
the structural stratum of memory are paranormally activated. The
nature of the ESP experience must necessarily depend also on the
mediation of the activated information into consciousness. It is therefore appropriate to consider now those processing loci which are
utilized in mediating *normally* activated memorial information into
consciousness, and to examine evidence of their involvement in
ESP.

It will be recalled that in normal reminiscence, only the processing locus of pattern recognition and those above it are employed
in mediating memorial information into consciousness. To the extent
that a memory model of ESP entails mediation of psi inputs by normal cognitive processes, it would be predicted that ESP does not
depend upon any locus below that of pattern recognition. Certainly
under a memory model the involvement of such loci is improbable,
for the following reason. Feature extraction and afferent storage appear to be contiguous processes (see Sakitt, 1976). If the features of
extrasensory information have in effect already been "extracted" in
the structural stratum of memory, these afferent processing levels of
the system would be redundant in the context of psi processing.
Further, as far as I am aware, there is no evidence of the involvement of such loci in ESP. This is not to say that there is little point
in trying to establish such evidence. On the contrary, investigation
of relationships between ESP and afferent processes would constitute one means of testing the memory model in its present form,

and hence it is in the interests of parapsychological science that such investigation be energetically pursued. For reasons indicated earlier, however, I doubt that these efforts would prove successful.

A more fruitful analysis of the dependence of ESP upon information processing loci is possible for the level of pattern recognition. At this locus of processing, preconscious recognition of (normal) inputs is achieved in terms of primitive structural features. If the systemic source of psi inputs comprises structural information, then logically the first step in mediating psi input into consciousness should be pattern recognition of this structural information.

What evidence is there that psi inputs are subject to the processes of pattern recognition? The relevant data concern the nature of erroneous responses in ESP tasks. As noted previously, errors tend to be of a structural type. This suggests that recognition of the extrasensory "pattern" may be marked by qualitatively poor matching of the input's primitive structural features against those of previously experienced patterns, such as might occur with very weak inputs.

If this interpretation is valid, it should be found that the "correct" and "incorrect" facets of the response can be unambiguously related to specific, very simple, primitive structural features of the target. It is possible to test this prediction, but a major obstacle has been the difficulty of comparing two given figures in terms of their primitive features. For example, the structural relationship between target and response may be extraordinarily subtle, especially when the subjects used in the study are not particularly "sensitive." Thus while the presence of such a relationship can be detected through application of special statistical techniques (see Thalbourne, 1978), we may be unable to reliably specify the relationship, let alone to formulate it in terms of primitive features. The problem persists even when the relationship is a more obvious one. For instance, as mentioned earlier, some striking structural similarities have been observed between pictorial targets and attempts by gifted subjects to draw these targets on the basis of extrasensory information (see, e.g., Warcollier, 1948). However, these pictures are generally so complex that it would be a daunting task to describe the observed structural relationships at the level of primitive features. To assess the above interpretation of the origin of structural errors, it is therefore necessary to examine the work of experimenters who have in some way solved the problem of comparing the structure of the response to that of the target.

One efficacious technique is the use of targets which are simple in structure: when the target and response figures are simple, their primitive structural features can be defined and compared more readily. In one early study of this type, Bender (1936) employed individual letters of the alphabet as targets in a task of clairvoyance with a gifted subject. It was found that the primitive structural features of incorrect responses were often similar to those of the target. For example, if the target was the letter Q, the subject would tend to respond with O, G, or C. Since the number of trials in this study was very small, these data are of limited evidential value when considered in isolation. Nevertheless Bender's observations are supported by independent observations of similar effects in extrasensory perception of structurally simple targets. Thus similarities at the level of primitive structural features are reported by Ryzl (1970, p. 120) to occur between targets and erroneous responses in a study of clairvoyant reading of printed text, and indeed also in studies using the standard ESP cards.

A possible limitation in this type of approach is that if structural similarities and distortions are observed with simple target material, by the very nature of the material these effects are likely to be in terms of primitive features. In other words, there is little scope for structural effects to occur at any more complex level. The above data therefore are consistent with the view that ESP involves pattern recognition of primitive structural features and that errors can result from inadequacies at this locus of processing, but the data may not be conclusive in this regard. Ideally what is required here is a slightly more complex target figure which can still be adequately defined in terms of primitive structural features, but which also permits at least the opportunity for structural comparisons to be made at more complex levels. If with this material effects are still limited to the level of primitive features, evidence for the involvement of pattern recognition processes in ESP would be all the stronger. Such a test has yet to be conducted. It might be noted that a technique devised by Harper (see Honorton, 1975b) could be extended to provide a means of generating target stimuli for this purpose.

Nevertheless there is one more particularly important piece of research which concerns the issue of ESP and pattern recognition. In an experiment conducted by Kelly, Kanthamani, Child, and Young (1975), a gifted subject tried to identify ordinary playing cards presented under two different experimental conditions. In one task each card was exposed very briefly by tachistoscopic projection on a screen. The second task was one of clairvoyance, with individual target cards placed inside an opaque folder. Confusion matrices were tabulated from the set of erroneous responses under each condition: that is, for each stimulus card the frequency of each incorrect response was recorded in one table for the "tachistoscopic" condition and in another for the "clairvoyance" condition. Now with tachistoscopic presentation, visual confusion errors are held to be due to the difficulty of pattern recognition of an item (Klatzky, 1975, p. 52): this is the result of the input's being "weak," in this case by way of its brief iconic (afferent visual) representation. In other words, pattern recognition here entails incomplete or otherwise inadequate comparison between the input's primitive structural features and those of stored patterns, and as a consequence the erroneously "recognized" pattern has some but not all of the features of the stimulus. The relevance of this point to the study by Kelly et al. is that these investigators found a strong resemblance between the confusion matrix for the ESP condition and that obtained under tachistoscopic presentation of stimuli. This result indicates the involvement of normal processes of pattern recognition in psi mediation. The data also provide additional support for the notion that in ESP, pattern recognition processes are applied to information whose systemic representation is in some sense weak.

It is clear that further research on this issue is warranted. Particularly deserving of attention is the matter of pattern recognition in extrasensory perception of nonvisual targets: we know very little about the characteristics of ESP with such target material. At the same time such evidence as is available does suggest that psi inputs are subject to pattern recognition.

In the normal course of processing, pattern recognition is followed by encoding of the preconsciously recognized information. It

is therefore pertinent to inquire if psi inputs also show evidence of
being encoded in their mediation to consciousness. The most reliably identified forms of coding are the visual code and the verbal or
"name" code. Is extrasensory information mediated by means of
such codes?

Examination of spontaneous psi experiences suggests that in the
majority of cases mediation of extrasensory input takes the form of
mental imagery, particularly visual imagery (Rhine, 1953, 1954;
Stevenson, 1970). Persinger's (1974) data suggest that about 60 per
cent of all spontaneous extrasensory experiences are mediated by
means of predominantly visual imagery. In introspective accounts of
psi processes, mediums and other gifted subjects also commonly report the use of visual images as a vehicle for psi reception (White,
1964). Such reports imply that visual encoding of extrasensory information may be a major factor in the mediation of this information
into consciousness.

Experimental investigations also evidence the role of visual coding in ESP, although there seem to be additional factors operating
which confound the precise nature of this role. Freeman (1970) has
demonstrated that the individual's spatial abilities are an important
determinant of that person's ESP scores. A similar observation in
children has been reported by Schmeidler (1962). To the extent that
factors in visual coding underlie individual differences in spatial
abilities, such results are favorable to our argument. One would expect a more definitive picture to emerge from tests involving some
measure of visual imagery, since the nature of a visual image in consciousness may be more intimately linked to visual coding than may
spatial ability. However, the results of studies relating ESP to vivid-

ness of mental imagery have thus far proved inconsistent. For example, Honorton, Tierney, and Torres (1974) report that subjects rated as vivid mental imagers showed psi-hitting, while a group of "weak" imagers showed psi-missing. On the other hand, contrary effects were observed in an attempted replication of this study by Schechter, Solfvin, and McCollum (1975), with "strong" imagers yielding a nonsignificant tendency toward psi-missing, and "weak" imagers psi-hitting to a significant degree.

One possible source of these discrepant results is the scale employed to rate the vividness of the subjects' mental imagery. In both studies the shortened form of the Betts QMI (Sheehan, 1967) was used for this purpose, and Honorton (1975a) has raised doubts about the construct validity of this scale. Additionally, the Betts QMI measures vividness of mental imagery in seven different sensory modalities, and the QMI score actually represents the summation of scores over the seven subtests. It is therefore possible that an individual may be identified on Bett's QMI as a "strong imager," yet because of highly vivid imagery in nonvisual modalities, he may in fact be a relatively weak *visual* imager. Hence, while the experimenters in each of the above studies may have reliably assigned subjects to experimental groups differing in vividness of mental imagery, differences between the groups in *visual* imagery may not have been consistent across the two studies. To the extent that ESP is critically dependent upon vividness of visual imagery rather than that of imagery in all sensory modalities, the discrepancy between the two sets of data may have arisen from this uncontrolled variable.

Another, probably more cogent, factor underlying the observed inconsistency concerns the subjects' dependence upon visual imagery as a mediating process. An individual rated on the QMI as a "strong" imager might not necessarily employ visual mediation habitually. Indeed the vividness of visual imagery may rate higher than that of his auditory imagery, yet the individual may adopt the cognitive style of a verbalizer. There is a need here for an investigation relating ESP performance to what Paivio (1971, p. 495) terms "habitual modes of thinking," that is, tendencies to rely either on visual coding to a greater extent than on verbal coding, or vice versa. There is some support for this type of approach in Assailly's (1963) study of individual differences in mediums.

The evidence reviewed thus far might be taken to suggest that ESP is mediated by exclusively visual means: pattern recognition seems to be based on visual structural features, and is followed by visual encoding and thence a conscious experience of visual imagery. However, while visual processes evidently do make an important contribution to ESP, they are not the only means of psi mediation. In the first place, the data discussed above were derived from situations in which the ESP targets were typically of a pictorial nature. It is plausible that the type of information in the psi input does have an important bearing on the means of mediating that information into consciousness. Secondly, it is a fact that nonvisual experiences of ESP do occur. For example, cases of "intuitive" ESP involve imageless mediation and are commonly associated with a conscious experience of a verbal type (Stevenson, 1970). Indeed Persinger (1974) reports that in about 20 per cent of cases psi information is mediated into consciousness in an auditory, usually verbal, form. Such case material indicates the significance of verbal or "name" coding in psi mediation.

However, there is a regrettable lack of *experimental* data on verbal mediation in ESP. In part this is due to the fact that visual mediation appears to underlie the majority of cases of spontaneous ESP and has therefore been regarded as a more profitable avenue for research than has verbal mediation. Additionally the recent psychological fad of relating cognitive functions to one or other of the two cerebral hemispheres has left its mark on parapsychological research. Thus there have been various attempts to relate ESP to activity of the right, "nonverbal," hemisphere of the brain (see, e.g., Broughton, 1975), to the neglect of verbal functions. Nevertheless Maher and Schmeidler (1977) have restored some interest in the involvement of the more verbally proficient left hemisphere in psi mediation. These experimenters devised an ESP task in which there was an opportunity for functions of the left hemisphere to demonstrate their efficacy as vehicles for ESP. In the experimental condition of relevance here, the ESP targets were words, and each subject responded to the ESP task with his right hand (which is controlled by the left hemisphere of the brain). The right hemisphere was diverted with a spatial task. Significant ESP scores were observed under these conditions, suggesting that verbal encoding of information can serve an important role in psi mediation, particularly when the nature of the task makes such mediation conducive to better performance.

Reasonable empirical grounds therefore exist for assuming the dependence of ESP on the locus of input encoding. Of course in addition to defining the form of conscious mental experience, encoding processes serve to mediate semantic analysis of information. This appears to be as much the case in paranormal cognition as in normal cognitive processing. That semantic analysis is applied to psi inputs is evident from the fact that the individual generally comprehends the meaning (although not necessarily the significance) of the extrasensory information of which he becomes conscious. To this extent the involvement of the locus of semantic processing in ESP requires no further substantiation.

At the same time it is notable that semantic analysis of psi inputs is not limited to the extraction of denotative features. Indeed the input's connotative features seem to be a critical factor in performance on an ESP task. The connotative dimension of evaluation seems to be particularly pertinent: thus performance is differentially affected by the input's emotionality for the individual (e.g., Carpenter, 1971) and by the subject's like or dislike of the target material (e.g., Nash and Nash, 1968). The effect of such variables as these may be to enhance ESP, to prevent the information from reaching consciousness, or to produce psi-missing. For example, consider the case where a subject's intentional responses on an ESP task are at a completely chance level, that is, psi inputs presumably have not reached the level of consciousness. A number of studies (e.g., Dean, 1966; Tart, 1963; Schouten, 1976) have employed autonomic psychophysiological measures to demonstrate that at a preconscious level of processing, such a subject may in fact have extracted the input's connotative features and at least at this level has "identified" the input as a conflict-arousing one. Semantic analysis of connotative features is therefore a significant facet of psi processing.

Another characteristic of semantic processing of extrasensory information is that it may be incomplete. For example, in some spontaneous cases the experience is limited to an emotional reaction: the percipient may feel apprehensive or sorrowful, yet have no immediate appreciation of the reason for his reaction. In other words, connotative information may reach consciousness without concomitant denotative information. This may reflect the operation of defensive processes at some stage during semantic analysis: thus if the input's connotative features identify it as a traumatic one, further extraction of (denotative) features may be inhibited. In this regard it is interesting to recall that data reported by Wickens (1972) suggest that the evaluative dimension may be one of the first classes of semantic features to be elaborated.

If semantic information is admitted to consciousness the percipient will have some appreciation of the nature of the psi input. However, unless this information is also accompanied by visually and/or verbally coded information about the input, the ESP experience will be vague and lack contextual form. Hence, even if a subject's specification of an ESP target is incorrect, there may still be some semantic similarity between target and response (Rao, Morrison, Davis, and Freeman, 1977).

The locus of memorial processes may also be involved in psi processing. Processes associated with primary memory are clearly implicated when the individual becomes aware of extrasensory information: primary memory is held to be the seat of consciousness in the information processing system. Since the states of consciousness associated with ESP are also found in normal cognition, it is a plausible assumption that primary memory is the locus of consciousness for psi inputs. Similarly, when the percipient is able to recall the ESP experience at some later time, secondary memory is utilized. In other words, information extracted from the psi input may be subject to further memorial processes which establish it as a more durable trace. Again there is no evidence to suggest that other than normal processing mechanisms are involved at this stage.

The matter of response processing in ESP warrants discussion in slightly greater detail. There are some situations in which psi is evidenced not as a conscious mental event but as a response. For example, the individual may report an experience of being suddenly immobilized or of performing some apparently irrational action. In these cases the individual is not immediately aware of any justification for such behavior and often has little volitional control over it. Certain automatisms performed by mediums may fall into the same category. It is possible that these paranormal experiences entail subconsciously mediated responses to psi inputs. To the extent that this is the case, the experiences can be accommodated in an information processing framework: as we have seen, there are occasions in normal cognitive processing when responses are made on the basis of semantic information which does not proceed beyond a preconscious level. It may be possible, then, to relate these subconsciously mediated paranormal responses to the normal response processing mechanisms of cognitive response determination, response program selection, and response execution. On the other hand it is also conceivable that some instances of this type of response are produced directly by paranormal means, that is, without any processing of extrasensory information by the respondent. Such direct effects would fall into the category of psychokinetic phenomena. An information processing approach to these phenomena is explored in Chapter 7.

Judging from cases of spontaneous ESP it is more typical for re-

sponses to be made on the basis of consciously perceived information. Admittedly this information may be very limited: the experience may consist of little more than awareness of an intuitive need
to perform a particular response. Nevertheless, where the response
is based upon consciously perceived information the situation is essentially the same as in normal cognitive processing. In other words
there is no need to appeal to any paranormal mechanisms in order
to account for responses to consciously perceived extrasensory information. This is not to deny that defensiveness, from both conscious and preconscious sources, may be an important factor in the
selection of a response to such information. Most people are self-
conscious to some degree and will usually choose a response that
neither they nor observers would regard as too irrational or eccen-
tric.

Documentation of the involvement of the information processing system in ESP therefore varies in quality from locus to locus.
Experimental evidence ranges from strongly supportive to almost
circumstantial, from thorough and extensive to virtually nonexistent.
There is nevertheless sufficient data upon which to base an information processing model of ESP, provided due recognition is given to
the fact that the principal function of a model is to generate further
research rather than to offer definitive resolution of all pertinent issues. In this particular case the available data suggest, first, that extrasensory inputs have their systemic source in memory, and second, that the processing loci involved in normal mediation of memorial information into consciousness are also involved in paranormal
cognition. A model of ESP will now be formulated to accord with
these principles.

A *Model of Paranormal Cognition*

In this section we will speculate beyond the confines of currently available experimental evidence and develop a model of the
involvement of the human information processing system in
paranormal cognition.

The approach formulated below is a memory model of ESP. It
should be noted, however, that the model does not make a distinction between activation of target-relevant memory traces by unknown, paranormal means and their activation by a psi stimulus
which enters the human information processing system at the level
of memory. Trace activation may simply "happen" (Gauld, 1976) as,
for example, the result of teleological causes (Edge, 1978), or it may
be a consequence of some type of environmental stimulus entering
the system. To a large degree this distinction is not necessary to an
account of processing of extrasensory information, although some
would argue that only the former approach can account for precognition (e.g., Kelly et al., 1975, p. 27; Randall, 1975, p. 94). This is not
to say that the issue underlying the difference between these two
approaches is unimportant, but merely that its resolution one way or
the other could be accommodated within the model below, without
affecting the basic arguments. The term "psi input" may be interpreted to imply either approach: it simply designates that information contained in the activated memory traces. The relationship between the psi source (in the environment) and the psi input (in the
memory system) is termed *concordance,* or as Stanford (1977, p.
371; 1978) prefers, conformance. Again this descriptive nomenclature should not be taken to imply any particular mode of trace acti-

vation: concordance may be due to either physical or teleological causes.

The model will be formulated initially in the context of an individual who has no expectation of nor "striving" for a psi experience. There is extensive evidence that ESP can occur without conscious effort or awareness of the existence of the situation to which the extrasensory information refers (see Schechter, 1977, or Stanford, 1974a, for a review). This type of paranormal cognition is known as *nonintentional* ESP. Hence the initial description of the model would be applicable to many spontaneous cases and to empirical studies of nonintentional ESP.

Receptive processes in the information processing system begin with the formation of a concordance relationship, that is, activation of secondary memory traces which are "relevant" to the psi-source or target. Such "relevance" is in structural terms, because the activated memory traces are in the structural stratum of secondary memory and take the form of coded representations of inputs' primitive sensory features. In this process it is possible that fragmentation, disorganization, and distortion may occur. For example, if the target was a picture of a bicycle, there is a chance that the memory trace (or trace network) corresponding to a *flower* might be activated also, since the radiating configuration of a flower is structurally relevant to the nature of a spoked wheel. Similarly, if the psi source is a word represented in purely auditory terms, activated traces may encode words rhyming with the target or having various other acoustic and articulatory similarities to it. Further, there may be more than one "relevant" trace thus activated, either concurrently or over the period of psi reception, and this may contribute to fragmentation.

The consequent instability of trace activation is the basic sense in which psi inputs are "weak."

Under a concordance relationship relevance may be determined in a purely objective, perhaps physical, fashion, as by a process similar to resonance (Marshall, 1960). It is also possible, however, that this facet of concordance could be at least supplemented by a subjective element. The assumption of subjective components in concordance would admit the operation of defensive processes even at this early stage of psi processing. For example, following the suggestion of Kreitler and Kreitler (1974, p. 282), some instances of psi-missing may stem from a tendency to determine relevance in terms of *negation*. Hence if the psi source is a circle, the traces activated in some individuals' memories may correspond to the information "non-circular"; consequently these individuals would make erroneous responses to psi sources more frequently than expected by chance.

Subsequent processing of this memorial information will depend upon the allocation of processing capacity to such inputs. Allocation of capacity to psi processing will be governed by a number of factors, such as the extent to which concurrent cognitive and motor activities are attention-demanding, and the individual's defensiveness in processing information from paranormal sources.

If the individual is preoccupied with normal cognitive processing and psi inputs can not be immediately processed, the information may possibly be processed at some later time. In the most common situation of this type, the psi event occurs during the day when the individual is too busily engaged in work to deal with such inputs. That night, however, the extrasensory information may emerge in consciousness in the form of a dream. It seems that the recency with which memory traces were activated is encoded in memory. Thus during the night, when the processing system is relatively free of the cognitive demands of modern life, traces activated earlier that day can be located and, if sufficiently important, brought to the individual's attention during his dreams (and nightmares). This function of dreaming relates also to psi-activated memory traces (see Freud, 1922). The period between the occurrence of the psi event and that of the individual's conscious psi experience is termed the *latency* of ESP (Warcollier, 1948).

For the purpose of further description it will be assumed that the individual is in a psi-conducive state, thereby ensuring the immediate availability of sufficient capacity for at least some of the subsequent stages of processing.

As postulated above, psi-activated traces consist of coded representations of the primitive sensory features of a particular input (or inputs) with some structural relevance to the psi source. At the next stage of processing, this set of primitive sensory features is subjected to the preconscious processes of pattern recognition. This locus is the first stage in the mediation of psi inputs into consciousness, or at least in their mediation toward that level of the information processing system. In pattern recognition a selection among possible alternative interpretations of an input is normally required. For example, the primitive structural features defining a "B" to some extent overlap those defining an "8." Hence a psi input which has these common features could potentially be recognized as either B or 8, and a selection must be made at this locus of processing. The difficulty of this process of selection is compounded by the typically weak state of the psi input: during the period of psi reception a variety of "relevant" traces may be activated, both intermittently and concurrently, so that the set of features to be recognized at this locus may be unstable and indefinite.

Usually the process of selection among alternative patterns is markedly affected by sets, expectancies, and contexts. These factors are likely to be of limited importance in nonintentional ESP. Nevertheless selection among patterns can still be a significant opportunity for defensiveness to operate. This may be achieved by choosing as the "recognized" pattern one which has less than the greatest number of features in common with the input. Suppose, for example, that the letter B was the psi source. Even if this input has not been substantially affected by defensiveness in the process of concordance, the "recognized" pattern may in fact be taken as "8," or even more harshly, as "I." In pattern recognition, therefore, there is a further potential source of interference with the veridicality of ESP.

The information "recognized" at this preconscious level of processing may then be coded in a form appropriate for its semantic analysis. Both a visual code and a name code may be established. Although formation of these codes does require processing capacity (Comstock, 1973; Millar, 1975; Shwartz, 1976), there does not seem to be any circumstance in which one code is established at the exclusion of the other. The dominance of one particular code at subsequent stages of psi processing therefore may stem not from any restriction of encoding to this one form, but from the relative efficiency in extracting this code with the given type of psi input, and from the individual's cognitive style or habitual tendency to employ this type of code to mediate processes at subsequent loci.

Encoded extrasensory information may next be subject to preconscious semantic analysis. One of the first semantic features to be elaborated relates to the connotative dimension of evaluation, that is, the information's pleasantness or unpleasantness for the individual. If the psi input is identified here as emotionally disturbing, defensive processes may again be applied, with various possible effects. Further (denotative) semantic analysis may be aborted, so that the subject may become aware only of an unspecific emotional reaction. In a more extreme case, all information extracted from the input may be prevented from reaching the level of consciousness. Alternatively a semantic code which is contrary to the content of the input may be established: this may be another source of psi-missing.

The admission of extrasensory information to primary memory and consciousness is by no means automatic. In the case of nonintentional ESP, if the semantic content of the psi input is lower in subjective importance or interest than other concurrently processed information, it may simply remain unattended and the individual will have no conscious appreciation of its existence (see Braud, 1975, p. 150). Even if the extrasensory information is of some relevance to the individual, its admission to consciousness may be affected by further defensive operations, such as distortion of the content of the experience and partial or complete repression of the information. On the other hand, if the individual's defensiveness is sufficiently low and the importance of the psi input sufficiently high, extrasensory information may be admitted to consciousness in a relatively veridical state.

The form of the conscious ESP experience will generally depend upon the code employed for mediating semantic analysis of extrasensory information. Thus if a given code has reached the level of semantic processing, it may accompany the entry of semantic information into consciousness, thereby giving context to the experience. As noted previously, the code used in such mediation is in part a function of the individual's cognitive style. Individuals who are habitual visualizers will therefore tend to have visual ESP experiences. The form of the experience will be governed also by the current cognitive state of the individual. For example, verbal encoding might be more common during normal waking activities in which visual components of the processing system are involved in environmental monitoring: here ESP might take the form of an imageless intuition or an auditory hallucination. Similarly, when visual contact with the environment is minimal, as during sleep or reverie, the visual code may be used; the psi experience in this case could be a telepathic dream or a visual hallucination.

It is also possible for a given code to reach the level of semantic analysis and to serve its mediating role at this locus, but then fail to accompany semantic information into consciousness. With neither visual nor verbal codes in consciousness to give the ESP experience some structural context, the percipient will have nothing more than a vague and formless notion of the meaning of the input. Hence he may be completely unable to specify the psi source, yet still show an inclination to make responses semantically associated with it.

Processing of consciously perceived psi information would be similar in most respects to that in any normal conscious experience. Nevertheless two points of qualification should be noted. Firstly, the salience and vividness of an ESP experience may enhance the probability of its secondary storage and the ease of its retrieval from memory. Secondly, in cases where the individual has the opportunity to report the experience to others, retrieval and response processing may be subject to further defensive effects, from both conscious and subconscious sources.

Psi information may be prevented from reaching consciousness by the processing demands of other concurrent activities. In such circumstances it is nevertheless possible that semantically analyzed extrasensory information may be mediated at a subconscious level to initiate response processes. This type of psi experience takes the form of ostensibly causeless motor behavior: the individual may suddenly feel immobilized, he may appear to be pushed to one side by an unseen force, or he may perform some action over which he has little or no volitional control.

This, then, is the proposed course of processing where the percipient has no particular expectation of a psi experience. Of course in many situations, especially in experimental studies, ESP is intentional and psi processing is therefore subject to the effects of expectations. These effects will now be considered.

At a global level the principal effect of expectations on processing is the introduction of a conceptually driven or *top-down* processing program (Norman, 1976). This type of processing strategy was described in Chapter 3. Thus in intentional ESP, information is not left to work its way up through the system in the manner proposed above for nonintentional ESP. Under top-down processing, information on the range of expected inputs (e.g., the five standard ESP symbols) is maintained at a high level of the system, often in consciousness. This information is taken *down* through the system in search of any confirmatory evidence at lower loci that such input may be present. For example, the possibility that the target is a square is tested by searching at lower levels of processing for the registration of a particular configuration of lines or structural features consistent with such a target. In intentional ESP tasks these conceptually driven processes merge with the usual *bottom-up* processes in the mediation of information paranormally activated in memory.

The effects of top-down processes are felt particularly at the locus of pattern recognition, where a choice must be made between alternative interpretations of input. Hence, although the information reaching this level of the system may no longer be veridical, successful "recognition" can occur if one of the alternative interpretations still has a sufficient number of individual primitive structural features in common with the correct member of the set of expected targets. This is supported by MacFarland and George's (1937) observation that performance in an ESP card-guessing task is not affected by distortion of the symbols.

Certain aspects of capacity allocation in intentional psi are also distinctive; these are taken up in detail in Chapter 8. In these and other respects, therefore, there are some fundamental differences between processing programs for intentional and nonintentional ESP. Of course they still have in common the point of initial psi activation of the information processing system. Additionally the same sources and types of defensiveness may affect the course of processing under either program, although defensiveness at a conscious level can be greater in the case of intentional ESP.

In this chapter a specific memory model of paranormal cognition has been formulated. It must again be emphasized that in its present form the model goes beyond the available evidence. As the review of the literature in this and earlier chapters has shown, the model certainly does not lack empirical foundation. Nevertheless more research is clearly warranted. A major objective in constructing this model has been the provision of a context within which further research may be generated. It is therefore hoped that the information processing approach to ESP will prove both instructive and productive.

Chapter 7

PSYCHOKINESIS AND THE
INFORMATION PROCESSING SYSTEM

The possibility of modeling psi in information processing terms
has been demonstrated for the case of ESP. If such an approach is
applicable to what might be called the "receptive" aspects of psi, it
is pertinent to explore its applicability to psi phenomena that have
an ostensibly "output" character. In this chapter the nature of
psychokinesis (PK) is examined in relation to human information
processing.

Literally interpreted, the word *psychokinesis* means movement
by the mind or psyche. Thus many psychokinetic events involve
visible positional changes in physical systems. On the other hand PK
may also operate at a molecular or even subatomic level, and its effect may be evidenced not by visible movements as such but by a
change in the structure of a physical system. In essence, then, PK is
a "mind over matter" phenomenon: the individual can influence
matter by some paranormal, nonmechanical means which do not entail the known muscular effectors. Claimed forms of PK include
teleportation of objects, faith healing, psychic surgery, dowsing, poltergeist activities, stoppage of a clock or dislodgment of an object at
the very time of death of a close friend or relative, psychic photog-

raphy, levitation, the metal-bending feats of Uri Geller and other individuals, and various seance phenomena of physical mediums.

The currently most productive techniques in experimental investigation of PK involve electronic devices as the "targets" for psychokinetic action. These devices, designed to produce random series of events, are known as random event generators (REGs). Hence if a subject can successfully "will" a significant deviation from randomness in a series generated by a REG, PK is held to have occurred.

Psychokinesis therefore appears to be a kind of *paranormal output* phenomenon. However, there is no more justification for this view than there is for interpreting ESP as paranormal reception of an environmental stimulus. In both ESP and PK, concordance or conformance between an environmental state and a mental state may simply "happen." That is, concordance may stem from teleological rather than physical causes. In this sense there may be no actual output from the individual during the occurrence of a psychokinetic event. Irrespective of this it is legitimate to inquire, as we did with ESP, if there are identifiable cognitive processes which make an essential contribution to psychokinetic performance.

Much less is known about the nature of PK than about ESP. This necessarily limits the evidential foundations of an information processing model of PK phenomena. Nevertheless, provided this model is consistent with the available data, its formulation is certainly legitimate. Indeed, since PK is currently so little understood, the model may well serve the positive functions of generating testable predictions and providing a meaningful framework for further research. It is within this context that the following analysis is offered.

One respect in which PK may involve the information processing system concerns the extent to which PK performance relies on
processing of extrasensory information for its guidance. In the very
first experimental report on psychokinesis (Rhine and Rhine, 1943) it
was assumed that ESP must be employed preconsciously to determine the state of the target system throughout the period of the experimental trial and thereby guide the application of the psychokinetic "force" to achieve the desired outcome. However, there is little
empirical evidence that PK requires guidance of the sort originally
envisaged by the Rhines. In any event in relating PK to the human
information processing system our central concern is not with receptive processing of feedback information but rather with any systemic
functions that may be necessary for the actual production of
psychokinesis.

Perhaps the most basic implication of recent studies of PK is
that the phenomenon is *goal-oriented* (e.g., Schmidt, 1974; Stanford, 1977). Specifically, PK is dependent upon the arousal of a need
to which the outcome of psychokinetic action is relevant. In the case
of intentional PK the need may be for self-achievement or for a favorable reaction from the experimenter. Similarly a need state may
be evoked even when the individual is unaware of the task, that is,
in nonintentional PK. In some experimental investigations of nonintentional PK the relevant need is manipulated by the experimenter
before the task commences; in other studies a need-arousing situation is created and the subject apparently establishes its existence by
extrasensory means. Given this characteristic of PK, what information processing occurs in fulfilment of the need through successful
PK performance?

A significant aspect of such fulfilment is the *conceptualization* of a specific change in the environment which would satisfy the need aroused in the individual. The human information processing system would of course play an essential role in the goal conceptualization phase of PK. The nature of this role is evidenced in a study by Stanford (1969), in which the experimenter attempted to induce two different processing programs designed to achieve goal conceptualization in a task of intentional PK. In one experimental condition subjects were instructed to visualize the target on each trial: this encourages the formation of a visual code and its (type I) rehearsal in primary memory. Another processing strategy termed "associative activation" was employed in a second condition. Under the latter strategy subjects gave free associations to the target before each trial. This would put emphasis on semantic elaboration in goal conceptualization; additionally, since associative activation proceeded for two minutes before each trial, under this condition it is likely that the target was maintained in memory as a verbal code rather than as a visual code, the former being much easier to rehearse than the latter. Stanford found that individuals whose thought processes were normally dominated by vivid visual imagery obtained higher PK scores under the "visualization" condition, whereas subjects who were not so habitually reliant on visual mediation showed superior PK performance under the "associative activation" condition.

These results are in part confirmed by Krieger (1977), who reports a significant correlation between scores on an intentional PK task and the individual's inclination towards spatial, right hemisphere processing. It seems then that PK is linked in some way to the cognitive style of the individual. When someone employs his habitually preferred coding process in mediating goal conceptualization, PK is enhanced. Now, in the case of intentional PK the ostensible objective of such processes is to represent the goal of the PK task as a particularly salient trace in primary memory (consciousness). Is this the state of the information processing system that is critical to the occurrence of PK?

The answer to this is a definite "no." Psychokinesis can occur without a conscious percept of the goal to be attained or even awareness of the situation to which the goal pertains (Stanford, Zenhausern, Taylor, and Dwyer, 1975). On these grounds it might be argued that the apparent involvement of information processing in intentional PK is artifactual: it may be necessary to the individual's conscious perception of the task, but this factor is inessential and indeed irrelevant to the actual production of psychokinesis. It is certainly an inescapable conclusion that representation in primary memory is not necessary for PK. Nevertheless it is possible that this locus of processing is not the final stage of involvement of the human information processing system in intentional PK. Perhaps consciousness is but one of a number of optional routes to some locus which is ultimately responsible for the phenomenon of psychokinesis. Resolution of this issue might be expected to lie in an analysis of nonintentional PK.

Although increasing research effort is being devoted to nonintentional PK the results as yet are meager. Much of the experimentation has been intended merely to establish the existence of the phenomenon, both in humans (e.g., Stanford, Zenhausern, Taylor, and Dwyer, 1975) and in other animals (e.g., Schmidt, 1970). Detailed work is still to be done on correlating nonintentional PK with functions of the human information processing system. However, some suggestive evidence is reported by Krieger (1977). She observed a significant correlation between nonintentional PK performance and scores on a test which measures depth of semantic processing. This is a most interesting result in view of the fact that depth of semantic processing is a determinant of the strength of a trace not so much for the purposes of primary memory but for those of *secondary* memory. Krieger's data therefore might be interpreted as indicating a relationship between PK and the extent to which the individual tends to process information in such a way as to increase the likelihood of its secondary storage.

It may be injudicious to place too much weight on the result of a single experiment: Krieger's (1977) study does warrant independent confirmation. At the same time the link between PK and secondary memory is a meaningful concept in a number of respects. Consider first the data cited above for intentional PK, which suggested that performance reflected the strength or clarity with which the individual represented the goal in primary memory. This can now be seen not merely as ensuring the subject's awareness of the task but also as a means of enhancing the probability that goal conceptualization passed from primary to secondary representation. In these terms both intentional and nonintentional PK would entail formation of some type of trace in secondary memory. The principal difference between the two varieties of PK performance is that in one case information is mediated into secondary memory via consciousness, while in the other case such mediation is totally subconscious.

A further aspect of this view of PK arises from consideration of the kind of information in secondary memory that might be critical to the occurrence of psychokinetic phenomena. At present there is no definitive evidence on this issue. Hence, for example, we do not know the extent to which errors in PK performance tend to be structural, referential, or semantic distortions of target information. It must be said that the typical PK study with its use of numerical targets has limited potential for investigation of errors in these terms. At the same time some data of possible relevance may be mentioned here. Eisenbud (1977) has described the nature of certain erroneous responses in a rather controversial PK task, namely that of psychic photography. This task entails the production of a photographic image of a given target by psychokinetically affecting unexposed film. Eisenbud (1977, pp. 426–427) reports that some semantic distortions did occur when the subject misperceived the target, that is, when his concept of the PK goal was a semantic transformation of the actual target. More significantly, in a number of cases the photographic response was structurally disorganized and distorted in relation to a drawing of the target made by the subject. This might be interpreted as suggesting that responses in a PK task exhibit structural associations with the individual's concept of the goal. However, these are tenuous grounds on which to argue that PK stems from a *structural* trace in secondary memory. Not only is psychic photography a controversial phenomenon in itself, but in some respects it is not really representative of psychokinetic phenomena in general. Thus further investigation is needed to determine the kinds of errors that can occur in PK tasks.

On the other hand in the information processing model of ESP it was postulated that the structural stratum of secondary memory was the initial systemic point of activation. It might be suitably parsimonious therefore to adopt as a working hypothesis the notion that in its "output" functions, psi has as its *final* systemic point of activation a structural secondary trace. Under this view the two general classes of psi phenomena are united: both ESP and PK feature concordance (or, conformance) between an environmental situation and a trace (or trace network) in the structural stratum of secondary memory. Such concordance may or may not be physically mediated, but it should certainly be regarded as a causal relationship (see Beloff, 1977, 1978). Hence ESP and PK are in a sense symmetrical facets of psi, being distinguishable primarily in the causal direction of the concordance relationship.

It should be noted that in the case of PK, establishment of an efficacious concordance relationship does not presuppose goal conceptualization to be related to ultimate causal mechanisms. For example, in psychokinetic effects on a random event generator (REG) it is not necessary to assume that the individual has formulated, even subconsciously, the PK goal in terms of the electronic circuitry or quantum processes of the REG's internal machinery. It is probable that the goal here is encoded in terms of the *output* of the REG: thus the PK goal may be the display of a 3, or the onset of a light or heat source. In PK a concordance relationship is established between the outcome of mental processes in the human information processing system and the outcome of physical processes in the environment.

The information processing model of psychokinesis may be briefly summarized as follows. Consider first the case of intentional PK. Here a need is aroused in the individual by sensory means.

This results in the conscious conceptualization of a goal which, again on the basis of sensory information, the individual implicitly or explicitly feels would reduce or satisfy the aroused need. All processing to this point follows the principles of normal cognition. If the individual employs his most efficient or preferred coding processes to mediate the goal information into consciousness, its representation in consciousness (primary memory) may be sufficiently salient to initiate (type II) rehearsal processes which establish this information as a secondary trace. In nonintentional PK the need may be aroused by either sensory or extrasensory means. This also leads to conceptualization of a need-related goal based on extrasensory information. However, in the nonintentional case the results of semantic encoding of the PK goal remain at a subconscious level. Now, if the strength of the aroused need is sufficient, semantic elaboration of goal information may be extensive. This, either in itself or in conjunction with additional appropriate control processes, may achieve subconscious mediation of the information into secondary memory. In both intentional and nonintentional PK the goal information may be represented in various strata of secondary memory. Nevertheless the type of representation postulated to be of critical relevance to PK is that in the structural stratum. Psychokinesis may be described as the paranormal formation of a concordance relationship between the structural representation of the goal in memory and an arrangement of physical entities in the environment.

As has been acknowledged above, there is a dearth of definitive evidence for this model. At the same time much that is known about PK is certainly consistent with the information processing approach. Thus many of the characteristics of ESP are found also in PK. For

example, PK exhibits decline effects and other position effects
(Rhine, 1969). Like ESP, psychokinetic phenomena are not limited
by temporal restrictions (e.g., Schmidt, 1976). Psi-missing also occurs, that is, a subject's performance on a PK task may be significantly *poorer* than expected by chance (e.g., McMahan, 1947).
There are similarities between ESP and PK in regard to the
psychological conditions conducive to successful performance (Honorton, 1977). Such parallels between the two classes of psi
phenomena support the formulation of two structurally similar and
functionally related models to account for ESP and PK.

Another feature of PK that warrants comment in this context is
that conscious concentration to achieve the task may be self-
defeating. There is growing evidence that intentional PK performance is most successful when the individual wants to do well but
puts the task temporarily "out of mind" (see, e.g., Stanford and Fox,
1975). In other words the PK goal must be kept in memory, yet not
necessarily in primary memory (consciousness). One reason for the
effect may be that this strategy encourages retention of the information in secondary memory rather than in its mere maintenance in a
primary form. This is clearly consistent with the account of intentional PK outlined above, in which the involvement of secondary
memory was a crucial element. This is not to claim, of course, that
this is the only factor behind the so-called "release-of-effort" effect.
An additional element of the effect's bases will be considered in the
next chapter.

It is appropriate to conclude discussion of psychokinetic
phenomena with at least a brief reference to a further ostensibly
"productive" facet of psi, namely the contribution of an *agent* to

telepathic communication. The notion of an agent as the informational source in telepathy may in fact be a gross simplification of affairs. For example, the causal direction of the concordance relationship in this type of ESP may be much more of a two-way nature than such a notion would suggest (see Schmeidler, 1961). Indeed in some situations there is doubt as to whether the agent makes any positive contribution to ESP at all (Langdon-Davies, 1956). Nevertheless there is reason to believe that the agent can play an active role in establishing telepathic concordance. Thus there are cases in which individuals perform well in telepathic tasks but score at chance level under clairvoyant conditions, even when the subjects are kept blind as to the two conditions (e.g., Klein, 1971). Further, Kreitler and Kreitler (1973) observed significant hitting in a nonintentional ESP task when the agents were instructed to telepathically "send" the target information to the subjects, but not when the agents were asked to simply think about the information.

Now, it has been argued by Stanford (1974b) that the active psi contribution of a telepathic agent may be accommodated within the scope of psychokinetic phenomena. Under this view, therefore, the information processing model of PK is applicable to the telepathic functions of an agent. In other words, in establishing a concordance relationship with the percipient, the agent's contribution entails activation of a relevant trace in the structural stratum of his own memory. Some implications of this account will be discussed in Chapter 8.

While on the subject of the agent's performance, it is notable that successful agents tend also to be good percipients in ESP tasks (Warcollier, 1938, p. 275; Zotti and Cohen, 1970). This point provides some additional support for the formulation of structurally related models of ESP and PK.

The present analysis of PK is therefore consistent with the view that PK and ESP belong to the same phenomenal dimension. Under the information processing models of psi events, formation of a concordance relationship and the involvement of structural traces in secondary memory stand as the central elements of such phenomena.

After completing the manuscript of this book, the author conducted an experiment in which support was found for the memory model of PK. Here it was demonstrated that in a nonintentional PK task, representation of the goal state in secondary memory is a necessary condition for the occurrence of psychokinetic effects. Such secondary representation is, of course, not a *sufficient* condition; it is also necessary for a concordance relationship to be established between the relevant secondary trace-network and the target system.

Chapter 8

PSI AND THE HUMAN
INFORMATION PROCESSING SYSTEM:
FURTHER CONSIDERATIONS

In this book both ESP and PK have been modeled in information processing terms. However, these models have been formulated
on the basis of the particular individual loci of the information processing system that seem to be implicated in psi phenomena. Thus
far, insufficient attention has been given to holistic principles of the
system's operation and their relation to psi. If an information processing approach to paranormal phenomena is to prove meaningful,
it must take account of these holistic principles. For this reason we
now turn to an examination of psi processing in relation to the concepts of processing capacity and attention.

Chapter 3 introduced the notion of *processing capacity*. Thus
Kahneman (1973) proposes that the processes at many loci of the information processing system require "effort" or capacity for their
execution. The common pool of processing capacity upon which
these processes rely is, however, a limited resource. Control decisions are therefore required in order to regulate allocation of capacity among the sources of information present in the system at any
one time. Priority in capacity allocation is given to inputs to which
the individual is set to attend. Even when capacity demands of at-

tended tasks are substantial, however, there is an amount of "spare" processing capacity available to permit analysis of unattended information, at least to some degree. In this manner other potentially important or "relevant" inputs may be identified as such and attention switched to these where appropriate.

The allocation of processing capacity is a fundamental principle governing the global operation of the information processing system. Hence, if the information processing models of ESP and PK are viable, the applicability of Kahneman's (1973) capacity theory to psi phenomena should be examined. Let us first consider the position with regard to ESP.

Under the model of paranormal cognition outlined in Chapter 6, such processes as pattern recognition, encoding, and semantic analysis were critically implicated in psi processing. If this is the case, ESP should be associated with demands upon processing capacity. There has been little experimental work directly attacking this hypothesis. Nevertheless a number of studies have involved attempts to manipulate the difficulty of an ESP task and are thereby relevant to the idea that processing of extrasensory inputs calls for capacity. In one study Kanthamani (1974) investigated the performance of a single "gifted" subject on a standard card test of ESP conducted under conditions which the experimenter judged to be of increasing complexity. Scores under each experimental condition were significant, but no effect of task complexity was evident. However, the nature of the different experimental conditions requires comment. They entailed introduction of a different experimenter, increased separation of experimenter and subject, and use of successively more complicated methods of randomizing the target order.

These modifications in procedure from series to series would appear to have involved relatively little change in *processing complexity* as such. In terms of the information processing model, once concordance had been established and relevant memory traces activated, the nature of their processing would have been much the same under any of Kanthamani's experimental conditions. Consequently these results are inconclusive on the issue of capacity demands in the processing of psi inputs.

More recently Spinelli (1977) conducted a study of ESP performance employing a word-pairs vocabulary test as the primary task or ESP "vehicle." Processing demands associated with the primary task were manipulated through the complexity of association between matched words. As the complexity of the primary task increased, ESP scores were observed to fall significantly. Spinelli's data may be interpreted as follows. An increase in the complexity of the primary task would be accompanied by a greater demand upon the limited pool of processing capacity. There would be a consequent reduction in the "spare" capacity available for processing extrasensory information, thereby retarding ESP performance.

Another, though less direct, source of evidence on this issue concerns the nature of the cognitive states that are conducive to ESP. Considerable research has been devoted to the determination of activities which facilitate ESP and those which inhibit it. Some general trends in this research may be summarized. Sensory stimulation markedly interferes with psi processing; this can be overcome by various forms of sensory deprivation (Honorton, 1977) or by training in techniques which encourage the individual's attention to internal processes of mentation (Honorton, 1974). Nevertheless, mentation of a concentrated, analytic type should be minimal, although less effort-involving types such as dreams and fantasy usually facilitate ESP (Braud, 1975). Additionally, psi receptivity is retarded by somatic, muscular activity: hence training in relaxation techniques is found to improve ESP performance (Braud and Braud, 1973, 1974). These experimental results are supported by data from cases of spontaneous ESP which indicate that such experiences tend to occur while the percipient is engaged in cognitively undemanding or "automatic" activities (see Persinger, 1974, p. 69). In essence, then, the states that inhibit success in ESP tasks are associated with major demands upon processing capacity. This is consistent with capacity theory, for the following reason. If the individual is preoccupied with one of these highly attention-demanding activities, there may be a consequent insufficiency of capacity remaining for complete analysis of extrasensory information. Under these circumstances, in spite of the potential importance of the psi input, the amount of processing capacity that can be immediately allocated to this input may be so limited that the information simply can not be processed to such a high level of the system as primary memory (consciousness). In this regard, therefore, the nature of psi-conducive cognitive states supports the view that processing of extrasensory information is capacity demanding.

Additional evidential support is found in the work of Soal and Bateman (1950). Their "gifted" subject, Mrs. Stewart, performed a telepathic task with two or more agents who either *competed* by looking at different targets on each trial, or *cooperated* by looking at identical series of targets. Under the competitive condition, the subject appears to have selectively attended to one agent, achieving a significant score with that agent's targets and scoring at chance with the others. In the tests with cooperating agents, performance was no better than with one agent alone. These results are consistent with the hypothesis that psi processing does require capacity, and that for this reason only a limited amount of extrasensory information can be processed at any one time. Certainly, however, the role of capacity limitations in processing multiple psi sources warrants investigation with broader samples of both subjects and agents. This need is all the more pressing in the light of recent work in Britain (Markwick, 1978) which suggests that Soal tampered with the data in at least two sittings with his subject Basil Shackleton. While there is no direct evidence that records of Mrs. Stewart's sessions were similarly manipulated, the confidence that can be placed in any of Soal's work is necessarily undermined.

One of the principal correlates of capacity allocation is held to be the individual's level of arousal (Kahneman, 1973, pp. 17–24). Thus task performance continuously improves as level of arousal and allocation of processing capacity concomitantly increase to an optimal level. This principle of capacity theory may account for observations (e.g., Palmer, 1972) that the deviation of ESP scores from chance increases with the individual's emotional involvement in the issue of the existence of ESP. Level of arousal would rise with emotional involvement; hence those subjects who are most concerned over the issue of psi will have a greater amount of processing capacity to allocate to the ESP task. As a result the deviation from chance of these subjects' scores would be enhanced.

At the same time, under capacity theory it is also possible for allocation of capacity to a given input to be excessive. In situations

in which the individual's level of arousal is very high, performance
is typically poor. Kahneman (1973, pp. 37–42) accounts for this effect
by arguing that high arousal is associated with excessive allocation of
capacity to the input, with the result that processing becomes far too
selective and causes performance to deteriorate. Now, if the principles of capacity theory are applicable to psi processing, we would
therefore expect to find that subjects under high levels of arousal do
not perform well in ESP tests. Indeed this is frequently noted to be
the case. For example, Braud and Wood (1977, p. 411) cite interference to ESP from excessive striving for strong performance (see
also Scherer, 1948). Similarly Eysenck (1967) suggests that introverts
do not score as well as extroverts on ESP tests because introverts
exhibit habitually high levels of arousal.

Another postulate of capacity theory concerns the effects of
practicing a task. As a task is practiced and the individual becomes
increasingly more skillful, the task requires progressively less "attention" for its execution. Thus once an activity becomes automatic it
uses very small amounts of capacity. This may account for the fact
that psi processing by many mediums appears to be more efficient
when responses are made by way of motor automatisms. The lower
capacity demands of response processing with such automatisms may
be to the advantage of capacity allocation to the extrasensory information itself. In the case of automatic writing this account is rein-
forced by the work of Spelke, Hirst, and Neisser (1976), which
demonstrates that, with considerable practice, writing of meaningful
material can be performed with very little demand for attention and
apparently without conscious mediation.

A further characteristic of capacity allocation is that the individual develops certain habits in his capacity allocation policy; that is, priority in capacity allocation may be given to information from certain sources or of a particular type. This may have major implications for psi processing. For example, if the individual's capacity allocation policy is conditioned to be heavily biased against extrasensory inputs, there may be little chance that such information will be processed to a level where it could be selected for admission to consciousness. However, provided sufficient capacity is allocated to enable extrasensory information to be processed at least to the locus of semantic analysis, the input's importance to the individual can be assessed and some type of psi experience may eventuate. In this respect capacity allocation would be a basic determinant of the magnitude of an ESP score's deviation from chance level. The concept of "capacity allocation policy" may therefore have some explanatory value in attempts to account for individual differences in deviation scores.

On the basis of the preceding analysis it seems, then, that processing of extrasensory information is subject to at least one holistic principle of the system's operation: namely, the dependence of information processing upon a limited pool of processing capacity.

At the same time it should not be thought that all instances of processing interference in ESP stem from competition in capacity allocation. There is another type of interference to cognitive performance known as *structural interaction*. This, it will be recalled, involves interaction between inputs which simultaneously occupy the same processing locus. Such an effect in psi processing has been observed by Maher and Schmeidler (1977). In this study subjects were required to perform simultaneously a (normal) cognitive task and an

ESP task, each of which depended heavily on one of two particular classes of processing mechanisms (in this case correlated with cerebral laterality). Performance in the ESP task was significant only when the two tasks differed in the type of processing mechanisms upon which they made greatest demands, that is, when structural interaction was minimized. Additionally, the effects observed by Spinelli (1977), cited above, may have stemmed not only from competing demands for processing capacity but also to a minor extent from structural interaction.

Holistic principles of operation of the human information processing system are therefore relevant to the characteristics of "receptive" psi processing. Let us now consider the situation for "transmissive" aspects of ESP. Here it must be immediately acknowledged that surprisingly little research has been conducted on the role of the agent (as distinct from the experimenter) in psi effects (White, 1976). The present analysis is necessarily limited by this dearth of empirical data.

It was noted in the previous chapter that the agent can apparently make some positive contribution to telepathic performance. While this need not be taken to imply that the agent should be regarded as a "transmitter" of psi input, it does seem that his active cognitive involvement may be conducive to success on an ESP task. It might be assumed that this "active" contribution of the agent in some way strengthens the concordance relationship between agent and percipient, and that this makes the psi input more "salient" in the subject's information processing system. The latter effect would increase the likelihood of the input's selection for admission to consciousness. However, unless it is possible to specify the role of the

agent's information processing system in affecting strength of concordance, such an account of the agent's role explains very little. It
is tentatively suggested that the "active" approach entails increased
arousal, which in turn is associated with a concomitant increase in
capacity allocated to the agent's processing of target information. Increased capacity, at least up to a certain optimal level, would enable
more efficient processing of target information and thereby would affect the representation of this information in the structural stratum
of secondary memory. Under the information processing model of
productive aspects of psi (see Chapter 7), such secondary memory
representation plays a key role in establishing concordance. Precisely how secondary representation is affected by more efficient
processing of target information is not certain; there may be a variety of effects. Greater allocation of capacity may increase the veridical qualities of secondary representation, or in some sense increase
the level of its activation, or increase the duration of trace activation.
Any one or more of these factors may be responsible for enhancing
concordance between the agent's active structural memory traces
and those of the percipient. Again, what is entailed in "enhancing
concordance" is unknown. It should be noted, however, that this aspect of the psi process is not one to which the information processing approach is immediately pertinent.

The proposed role of arousal in active agent telepathy is supported by the fact that the agent's mood can affect performance
(e.g., Carlson, 1970). Ullman and Krippner (with Vaughan, 1973, p.
215) also point out that qualities of the agent which apparently facilitate ESP performance include interest, motivation, and the abilities
to concentrate intensely and to become emotionally involved in the

target. Such qualities are closely linked with the factor of level of arousal, and it is conceivable that their effects are mediated via capacity allocation in the agent's processing system.

If the agent's allocation of capacity to processing of target information is a significant factor in telepathy, it may be argued that a further principle of capacity theory should apply—that under conditions of excessively high arousal in the agent, performance will be less successful. Again there is scant evidence upon which to evaluate this prediction. Nevertheless a number of reports suggest that performance in a telepathic task is enhanced when the agent keeps the target information somewhat outside the sharp focus of conscious attention (see Roll, 1966, pp. 515–516 for a review). Although more systematic investigation of this effect is warranted, it is consistent with the idea that excessive allocation of capacity may adversely affect the agent's contribution in ESP. It should also be noted that this effect has certain similarities to the "release-of-effort" effect in PK, to be discussed below.

There is thus some slight support for the view that agent processes in ESP are to be understood not merely in terms of the involvement of particular individual processing loci, but also in terms of the global characteristics of the system's operation. The lack of decisiveness in this area is not due to any equivocality in the available data, but rather to the lack of empirical research on agent processes.

A psi "output" phenomenon which has been investigated more extensively is that of PK. For this reason the relevance of holistic processing principles to productive aspects of psi might be assessed more readily in the case of PK.

In considering PK in terms of capacity theory an initial point that must be emphasized is that this approach can be applicable only to processes of the information processing system that underlie PK performance. Capacity theory may not validly be employed in attempts to account for the amounts of *physical energy* ostensibly required for psychokinetic movement of objects. In seeking evidence that PK demands processing capacity, we must therefore examine performance on PK tasks that clearly entail differential *cognitive* complexity. For example, while it may seem in a sense "harder" to achieve PK with twelve heavy dice thrown simultaneously than with only two light dice, the difference between these two tasks is not unambiguously one of cognitive complexity.

When the problem is thus defined, as far as I am aware there are no studies which have examined PK performance under two (or more) different levels of processing demands. However, assuming PK to have been demonstrated in cognitively elementary dice-throwing tasks with just a single face as the target, there have been some investigations of performance under more demanding conditions. In one such study Humphrey (1947) simultaneously threw six red and six white dice on each trial with the dual goal of achieving both a high number of target faces with the dice of one color and a low success rate with the other dice. Both aspects of her objective were achieved at a high level of significance. Similarly Steen (1957) investigated performance on a cognitively challenging PK task in which success on each trial required complex coordination of the outcomes of three dice thrown simultaneously. Again PK scores were significant. Now, it is difficult to estimate the actual extent of effects of task complexity in these studies because of the lack of control conditions. At the same time these studies clearly demonstrate that high PK scores can be attained in tasks in which other concurrent demands on processing capacity are major. In other words, if we distinguish between the processes underlying PK itself and those processes involved simply in encoding and semantically analyzing the PK goal, the critical processes in PK evidently require very little capacity for their execution.

At first sight this conclusion may appear to be contrary to intuitive expectation. After all, one might ask, surely it would be more taxing for the mind to move physical objects than to perceive extrasensory information? However, such a query loses sight of the caution drawn above, that we must distinguish processing capacity utilized in the information processing system from the energy presumed to be responsible for the work done in psychokinetically displacing objects. Thus in terms of processing capacity it is feasible that the loci involved in processing extrasensory inputs collectively demand more capacity than those essential to PK processing. This is certainly reflected in the information processing models of psi outlined in preceding chapters of this book. As we have seen, an experience of ESP relies on processes at several different loci of the system. In PK such is not the case. The processes of encoding and semantic analysis involved in conceptualization of the PK goal are not, strictly speaking, entailed in the productive aspects of PK. Such coding processes relate to sensory or extrasensory information which simply sets the scene for PK; that is, these preliminary stages of information processing provide nothing more than the datum from which are initiated the processes responsible for the psychokinetic effect itself. Under the present model of PK, this psi phenomenon is

due to the formation of a goal-relevant trace in the structural
stratum of memory and to the maintenance of this trace in an active
state. It is solely in these memorial functions of the information processing system that PK may rightly be said to demand capacity.
Understandably, then, these demands upon processing capacity are
distinctly smaller than those found in ESP.

The hypothesis that capacity demands of PK are small nevertheless warrants further consideration with regard to other features of
the phenomenon. For example, under this hypothesis the association
between level of arousal and capacity allocation leads to the
additional prediction that successful PK performance could be attained at low arousal levels. What then is the evidence concerning
PK and arousal?

In cases of nonintentional spontaneous PK, including nonrecurrent cases (Rhine, 1963) and poltergeist activity (Owen, 1964), there
is typically an emotional incident or problem which apparently insti-
gates the PK manifestation. However, the individual deemed to be
the "source" of the PK is not necessarily in an emotional or aroused
state at the time of the occurrence. Thus while the manifestation
may well reflect a strong need in the individual, his current state of
arousal may not be very high. A systematic study of nonrecurrent
spontaneous cases from this point of view is lacking. At the same
time it is notable that the cases described by Rhine (1963) do show
support for the hypothesis that PK can occur at low levels of arousal.
Of the cases in which Rhine reports the activity of the principal wit-
ness (the presumed PK "source") at the time of the incident, a high
proportion involve sources who were engaged in such activities as
sleeping, lying in bed, or sitting quietly. These activities are charac-

terized by low levels of arousal. Of course the sample of cases employed in Rhine's (1963) paper for illustrative purposes is not likely
to be a statistically random one. As a consequence it is not clear to
what extent a low level of arousal is actually conducive to (nonintentional) PK. Nevertheless there is certainly evidence here that PK
can occur under conditions of low arousal.

There are similar indications in cases of poltergeist activity. Indeed in his very exhaustive study of poltergeists, Owen (1964, pp.
359–360) concludes that hypnotic, hypnoid, hypnagogic, and "pre-
trance" states are all particularly conducive to poltergeist manifesta-
tions. Again these conditions are associated with very low levels of
arousal.

In nonintentional PK, therefore, there are reasonably strong indications that this phenomenon can occur when the source-
individual is in a state of low arousal. This is consistent with the
view that PK requires only small amounts of processing capacity: if
capacity demands in PK were considerable, the phenomenon simply
could not occur under conditions of low arousal. On the other hand
cases of nonintentional PK also suggest that low arousal is not a
necessary condition for the occurrence of PK. Thus in isolated instances nonintentional PK may be associated with an individual who
is somewhat aroused at the time of the incident. For example, Rhine
(1976, p. 162) cites one such case in which the apparent source-
individual was emotionally upset and was actually engaged in a particularly animated conversation when a PK event occurred. Now, if
PK does require only small amounts of processing capacity, it would
be expected that under conditions of moderate to high arousal,
capacity allocation would be excessive and PK performance would

thereby be adversely affected. How is it possible, then, for any case of PK to occur when the individual is in such an aroused state?

Before addressing this issue it may be pertinent to point out that these cases of nonintentional PK are spontaneous ones and hence are not based upon observation under controlled conditions. In such cases there will always be some element of doubt as to whether or not the incident was genuinely paranormal in nature. For this reason perhaps we should not give too much weight to these isolated cases that seem to be the exception to the rule. At the same time this hardly constitutes grounds for dismissing these discrepant cases out of hand. It is possible that the situation may be clarified by reference to further evidence, specifically in the context of intentional PK.

Much of what we know about intentional PK is derived from its investigation in the laboratory. Under such conditions arousal in intentional PK is likely to stem not so much from subconscious emotional sources as from conscious motivation to succeed. Confronted by an experimenter with a task upon which performance is to be scrutinized, measured, recorded, and ranked, typically the subject of a PK experiment would regard the situation as highly ego-involving. According to the present hypothesis, therefore, experimental investigation of intentional PK should be counterproductive. If PK demands relatively little processing capacity, and if under these highly arousing conditions allocation of capacity is excessive, performance should be inhibited.

Experimental data do tend to confirm this. It is clear that allocation of some processing capacity is required for success in an intentional PK task. Thus an *intention* to perform well is necessary (e.g., Gatling and Rhine, 1946). At the same time it does appear that intense striving can be counterproductive. A few of the supportive studies may be briefly mentioned. Camstra (1973) observed that subjects instructed to concentrate on the PK task performed poorly, whereas subjects who were not asked to concentrate were more successful. Similarly, Honorton and Barksdale (1972) found positive PK performance predominantly on trials in which subjects were instructed not to exert any effort to affect the outcome. The personality variable of *calmness* is also reported to be positively related to PK scores (Mischo and Weis, 1973). Stanford (1974b) has put forward a cogent case that ego-involved efforts to produce the desired outcome have an adverse effect on PK performance.

A phenomenon associated with the inhibition of intentional PK at high arousal levels is the so-called "release-of-effort" effect (Stanford, 1974b, 1977). This entails a tendency for hits on a PK target to occur immediately after that target has been abandoned. The release-of-effort effect has been noted incidentally in some PK experiments (e.g., Pratt and Woodruff, 1946). Additionally, a study designed specifically to investigate this effect was conducted by Stanford and Fox (1975), with results favorable to the hypothesis. The release-of-effort effect is consistent with the view that while the subject is highly aroused, PK performance is inhibited, but as soon as his intense concentration lapses, excess capacity allocated to PK processing is eliminated and PK is more likely to occur.

A good deal of data on intentional PK therefore support the hypothesis that PK demands little processing capacity. However, just as there seem to be isolated exceptions to this principle in cases of nonintentional PK, so too are apparent exceptions found in some observations of intentional PK. Thus PK performances by certain "gifted" psychics seem to be associated with fairly high levels of arousal. Perhaps the prime example here involves the Russian psychic Nina Kulagina. During Kulagina's production of psychokinetic feats, her muscles are tensed and her heart rate increases. At the end of long sessions a loss in body weight has been observed, and fatigue or even exhaustion is common (Pratt and Keil, 1973; Keil, Herbert, Ullman, and Pratt, 1976). These are clear indications of a state of high arousal. However, it has been suggested by Stanford (1974b, pp. 339–340) that such effects are merely part of a superstitious ritual performed by Kulagina in the mistaken belief that it is necessary for the occurrence of PK. Certainly there are other "gifted" individuals who have produced similar PK phenomena without exerting such apparent effort (see, e.g., Dierkens, 1978). It is possible that the excessive processing capacity associated with striving for success is channeled off into performance of the ritual itself, so that PK processes do not receive inhibitory amounts of "attention." In less technical terms, Kulagina's ritual may serve simply to keep her mind off the target objective without diminishing her intention to perform well.

Under this account, while a low level of arousal is both sufficient for and conducive to successful performance, PK can occur in states of higher arousal provided that the individual is engaged in activities which "drain off" the capacity in excess of that necessary for PK processing itself. The infrequent cases of spontaneous nonintentional PK which feature moderate to high levels of arousal can be accommodated satisfactorily under this account. Across a broad spectrum of data, therefore, it seems that the involvement of the information processing system in PK phenomena is accompanied by demands upon processing capacity, though to a relatively minor degree.

In both its "receptive" and "productive" facets, then, psi is subject to the holistic principles under which the human information processing system functions. This is an important result, for the following reason. In exploring the applicability of an information processing approach to psi phenomena, it is not sufficient merely to demonstrate that a given paranormal phenomenon is dependent on individual loci of the processing system. Rather it must be shown that such dependence forms a meaningful part of the whole system's involvement in psi. Now, the models of ESP and PK proposed in this book suggest how the operations of various loci are responsible for diverse characteristics of psi. The argument of the present chapter goes further in emphasizing that these operations occur in the context of a *system;* that is, psi experiences must be regarded as products of the information processing system as a whole and not as a net effect of a series of isolated, independent processes. The occurrence and nature of paranormal phenomena can only be understood with due appreciation of both the flow of information through the processing system and the factors that govern this information flow.

Reduced to its most basic form the thesis presented here is that the interaction between psi and the mind can be formulated in terms of the mechanisms and processes of normal cognition. It might be contended that this does not really account for psi. After all, you may argue, the explanation of psi lies in the determination of the nature of what I have termed *concordance;* indeed it would be surprising if the mental processes following concordance in ESP, or those preceding concordance in PK, were anything but a function of normal processing loci. To a degree this argument is valid. A major step will have been taken in solving the mystery of psi when we have a satisfying conceptualization of concordance, and as noted previously, this is not an issue to which an information processing approach is immediately applicable. Nevertheless the present thesis addresses itself to many other fundamental aspects of paranormal experience. It attempts to define the locus and state of the system to which the concordance relationship is relevant; or for those readers who favor an "information transfer" view of ESP and PK, the book might be interpreted as attempting to specify where psi information gets "into" or "out of" the system. Additionally, the *form* of the paranormal experience can be explained in terms of the processes of normal cognition, as can the origins of informational distortions that may occur in ESP. The information processing models of psi also provide a context within which the cognitive conditions of occurrence of paranormal phenomena may be investigated. This feature has particular significance: to the extent that it leads to greater control of psi phenomena it may permit more precise study of the nature of concordance.

While the present thesis does not presume to resolve all questions on paranormal phenomena, it surely addresses itself to a number of fundamental issues and hopefully will prove instructive in guiding at least the formulation of other questions in the future. At the same time it must be emphasized that the thesis comprises models, not specifications. Models should be explored, tested, and as new insights emerge, revised. Such is the intention here. I believe that the information processing approach will thereby make a positive contribution to progress in the science of parapsychology.

REFERENCES

Assailly, A. 1963. Psychophysiological correlates of mediumistic faculties. *International Journal of Parapsychology* 5(4): 357–373.

Atkinson, R. C., and Shiffrin, R. M. 1968. Human memory: A proposed system and its control processes. In *The Psychology of Learning and Motivation: Advances in Research and Theory*, vol. 2, K. W. Spence and J. T. Spence (eds.). New York: Academic Press.

Banks, W. P., and Barber, G. 1977. Color information in iconic memory. *Psychological Review* 84: 536–546.

Barber, T. X. 1971. Imagery and "hallucinations": Effects of LSD contrasted with the effects of "hypnotic" suggestions. In *Imagery: Current Cognitive Approaches*, S. J. Segal (eds.). New York: Academic Press.

Baron, J. 1973. Phonemic stage not necessary for reading. *Quarterly Journal of Experimental Psychology* 25: 241–246.

Bartram, D. J. 1976. Levels of coding in picture-picture comparison tasks. *Memory & Cognition* 4: 593–602.

Beloff, J. 1977. Psi phenomena: Causal versus acausal interpretation. *Journal of the Society for Psychical Research* 49: 573–582.

Beloff, J. 1978. Teleological causation. Paper presented at the Second International Conference of the Society for Psychical Research, Cambridge, England, March 28–30.

Bender, H. 1936. *Zum Problem der aussersinnlichen Wahrnehmung*. Leipzig: Barth.

Bergson, H. 1914. Presidential address. *Proceedings of the Society for Psychical Research* 27: 157–175.

Bierwisch, M. 1971. On classifying semantic features. In *Semantics: An Interdisciplinary Reader in Philosophy, Linguistics and Psychology,* D. D. Steinberg and L. A. Jakobovits (eds.). London: Cambridge University Press.

Blackmore, S. 1977. ESP: Perception or memory? Paper presented at the (first) International Conference of the Society for Psychical Research, London, April 14–17.

Bliss, J. C.; Crane, H. D.; Mansfield, K.; and Townsend, J. T. 1966. Information available in brief tactile presentations. *Perception & Psychophysics* 1: 273–283.

Bradshaw, J. L. 1975. Three interrelated problems in reading: A review. *Memory & Cognition* 3: 123–134.

Braud, L. W., and Braud, W. G. 1974. Further studies of relaxation as a psi-conducive state. *Journal of the American Society for Psychical Research* 68: 229–245.

Braud, W. G. 1975. Psi-conducive states. *Journal of Communication* 25 (1): 142–152.

Braud, W. G., and Braud, L. W. 1973. Preliminary explorations of psi-conducive states: Progressive muscular relaxation. *Journal of the American Society for Psychical Research* 67: 26–46.

Braud, W. G., and Wood, R. 1977. The influence of immediate feedback on free-response GESP performance during Ganzfeld stimulation. *Journal of the American Society for Psychical Research* 71: 409–427.

Broughton, R. S. 1975. Psi and the two halves of the brain. *Journal of the Society for Psychical Research* 48: 133–147.

Camstra, B. 1973. PK conditioning. In *Research in Parapsychology 1972,* W. G. Roll, R. L. Morris & J. D. Morris (eds.). Metuchen, N.J.: Scarecrow Press.

Carington, W. W. 1945. *Telepathy: An Outline of Its Facts, Theory, and Implications.* London: Methuen.

Carlson, M. L. 1970. Subject and "experimenter" moods and scoring on a correspondence ESP test. *Journal of Parapsychology* 34: 273–274.

Carpenter, J. C. 1971. The differential effect and hidden target differences consisting of erotic and neutral stimuli. *Journal of the American Society for Psychical Research* 65: 204–214.

Chari, C. T. K. 1967. ESP and "semantic information." *Journal of the American Society for Psychical Research* 61: 47–63.

Collins, A. M., and Quillian, M. R. 1972. Experiments on semantic memory and language comprehension. In *Cognition in Learning and Memory*, L. W. Gregg (ed.). New York: Wiley.

Coltheart, M. 1972. Visual information-processing. In *New Horizons in Psychology*, vol. 2, P. C. Dodwell (ed.). Harmondsworth, England: Penguin.

Comstock, E. M. 1973. Processing capacity in a letter-matching task. *Journal of Experimental Psychology* 100: 63–72.

Conrad, C. 1974. Context effects in sentence comprehension: A study of the subjective lexicon. *Memory & Cognition* 2: 130–138.

Craik, F. I. M., and Lockhart, R. S. 1972. Levels of processing: A framework for memory research. *Journal of Verbal Learning and Verbal Behavior* 11: 671–684.

Craik, F. I. M., and Tulving, E. 1975. Depth of processing and the retention of words in episodic memory. *Journal of Experimental Psychology: General* 104: 268–294.

Davis, J. C., and Smith, M. C. 1972. Memory for unattended input. *Journal of Experimental Psychology* 96: 380–388.

Dean, E. D. 1966. Plethysmograph recordings as ESP responses. *International Journal of Neuropsychiatry* 2: 439–446.

Delin, P. S. 1977. Two modes of ESP: A re-evaluation of the SRI experiment with Geller. *Journal of Parapsychology* 41: 77–78. (An abstract.)

Dick, A. O. 1971. On the problem of selection in short-term visual (iconic) memory. *Canadian Journal of Psychology* 25: 250–263.

Dierkens, J. C. 1978. Psychophysiological approach to PK states. In *Psi and States of Awareness: Proceedings of an International Conference held in Paris, August 24–26, 1977*, B. Shapin and L. Coly (eds). New York: Parapsychology Foundation.

Dixon, N. F. 1971. *Subliminal Perception: The Nature of a Controversy*. New York: McGraw-Hill.

Edge, H. L. 1978. A philosophical justification for the conformance behavior model. *Journal of the American Society for Psychical Research* 72: 215–231.

Ehrenwald, J. 1975. Cerebral localization and the psi syndrome. *Journal of Nervous and Mental Disease* 161: 393–398.

Ehrenwald, J. 1976. Parapsychology and the seven dragons: A neuropsychiatric model of psi phenomena. In *Parapsychology: Its Relation to Physics, Biology, Psychology, and Psychiatry*, G. R. Schmeidler (ed.). Metuchen, N.J.: Scarecrow Press.

Eisenbud, J. 1977. Paranormal photography. In *Handbook of Parapsychology*, B. B. Wolman (ed.). New York: Van Nostrand Reinhold.

Erdelyi, M. H. 1974. A new look at the new look: Perceptual defense and vigilance. *Psychological Review* 81: 1–25.

Eysenck, H. J. 1967. Personality and extra-sensory perception. *Journal of the Society for Psychical Research* 44: 55–71.

Feather, S. R. 1967. A quantitative comparison of memory and psi. *Journal of Parapsychology* 31: 93–98.

Freeman, J. A. 1970. Sex differences in ESP response as shown by the Freeman picture-figure test. *Journal of Parapsychology* 34: 37–46.

Freud, S. 1914. *The Psychopathology of Everyday Life*. London: Unwin.

Freud, S. 1922. Dreams and telepathy. *International Journal of Psycho-Analysis* 3: 283–305.

Gatling, W., and Rhine, J. B. 1946. Two groups of PK subjects compared. *Journal of Parapsychology* 10: 120–125.

Gauld, A. 1976. ESP and attempts to explain it. In *Philosophy and Psychical Research*, S. C. Thakur (ed.). London: Allen & Unwin.

Gurney, E.; Myers, F. W. H.; and Podmore, F. 1886. *Phantasms of the Living*, vol. 2. London: Trübner.

Haber, R. N. 1974. Information processing. In *Handbook of Perception. Vol. 1. Historical and Philosophical Roots of Perception*, E. C. Carterette and M. P. Friedman (eds). New York: Academic Press.

Hardy, A. C. 1950. Telepathy and evolutionary theory. *Journal of the Society for Psychical Research* 35: 225–238.

Honorton, C. 1972. Reported frequency of dream recall and ESP. *Journal of the American Society for Psychical Research* 66: 369–374.

Honorton, C. 1974. States of awareness factors in psi activation. *Journal of the American Society for Psychical Research* 68: 246–256.

Honorton, C. 1975a. Psi and mental imagery: Keeping score on the Betts scale. *Journal of the American Society for Psychical Research* 69: 327–332.

Honorton, C. 1975b. Objective determination of information rate in psi tasks with pictorial stimuli. *Journal of the American Society for Psychical Research* 69: 353–359.

Honorton, C. 1977. Psi and internal attention states. In *Handbook of Parapsychology*, B. B. Wolman (ed.). New York: Van Nostrand Reinhold.

Honorton, C., and Barksdale, W. 1972. PK performance with waking suggestions for muscle tension versus relaxation. *Journal of the American Society for Psychical Research* 66: 208-214.

Honorton, C.; Tierney, L.; and Torres, D. 1974. The role of mental imagery in psi-mediation. *Journal of the American Society for Psychical Research* 68: 385-394.

Humphrey, B. M. 1947. Simultaneous high and low aim in PK tests. *Journal of Parapsychology* 11: 160-174.

Hunt, E.; Lunneborg, C.; and Lewis, J. 1975. What does it mean to be high verbal? *Cognitive Psychology* 7: 194-227.

Irwin, H. J. 1976. Visual Selective Attention and the Human Information Processing System: Structures, Processes, and Processing Interference in Visual Input Selection. Ph.D. thesis, University of New England, New South Wales, Australia.

Irwin, H. J. 1978a. ESP and the human information processing system. *Journal of the American Society for Psychical Research* 72: 111-126.

Irwin, H. J. 1978b. Input encoding strategies and attenuation of Stroop interference. *Australian Journal of Psychology* 30: 177-187.

Irwin, H. J. 1978c. Psi, attention, and processing capacity. *Journal of the American Society for Psychical Research* 72: 301-313.

John, E. R., and Schwartz, E. L. 1978. The neurophysiology of information processing and cognition. *Annual Review of Psychology* 29: 1-29.

Johnson, M. 1968. Relationship between dream recall and scoring direction. *Journal of Parapsychology* 32: 56-57. (An abstract.)

Johnson, M. 1975. ESP and subliminality. *European Journal of Parapsychology* 1 [demonstration issue]: 9–18.

Johnson, M., and Kanthamani, B. K. 1967. The Defense Mechanism Test as a predictor of ESP scoring direction. *Journal of Parapsychology* 31: 99–110.

Johnson, M., and Lübke, C. 1977. A further attempt to validate the DMT as a predictor of scoring direction. *European Journal of Parapsychology* 1 (4): 37–46.

Kagan, J. 1966. Developmental studies in reflection and analysis. In *Perceptual Development in Children*, A. H. Kidd and J. L. Rivoire (eds.). London: University of London Press.

Kahneman, D. 1973. *Attention and Effort.* Englewood Cliffs, N.J.: Prentice-Hall.

Kanthamani, H. 1974. Psi in relation to task complexity. *Journal of Parapsychology* 38: 154–162.

Kanthamani, H., and Rao, H. H. 1974. A study of memory-ESP relationships using linguistic forms. *Journal of Parapsychology* 38: 286–300.

Kanthamani, H., and Rao, H. H. 1975. The role of association strength in memory-ESP interaction. *Journal of Parapsychology* 39: 1–11.

Keil, H. H. J.; Herbert, B.; Ullman, M.; and Pratt, J. G. 1976. Directly observable voluntary PK effects: A survey and tentative interpretation of available findings from Nina Kulagina and other known related cases of recent date. *Proceedings of the Society for Psychical Research* 56: 197–235.

Kelly, E. F.; Kanthamani, H.; Child, I. L.; and Young, F. W. 1975. On the relation between visual and ESP confusion structures in an exceptional ESP subject. *Journal of the American Society for Psychical Research* 69: 1–31.

Klatzky, R. L. 1975. *Human Memory: Structures and Processes*. San Francisco: Freeman.

Klein, J. 1971. A comparison of clairvoyance and telepathy. *Journal of Parapsychology* 35: 335. (An abstract.)

Klüver, H. 1930. Fragmentary eidetic imagery. *Psychological Review* 37: 441–458.

Kogan, I. M. 1966. Is telepathy possible? *Telecommunication and Radio Engineering* 21 (no. 1, part 2): 75–81.

Kreiman, N. 1975. Relationships between ESP and memory. *Journal of Parapsychology* 39: 362–363. (An abstract.)

Kreitler, H., and Kreitler, S. 1973. Subliminal perception and extrasensory perception. *Journal of Parapsychology* 37: 163–188.

Kreitler, H., and Kreitler, S. 1974. ESP and cognition. *Journal of Parapsychology* 38: 267–285.

Krieger, J. 1977. Hemispheric specialization in intentional versus nonintentional psi performance. Paper presented at the Southeastern Regional Parapsychological Association Conference, Greensboro, N. C. February 11.

Lackner, J. R., and Garrett, M. F. 1973. Resolving ambiguity: Effects of biasing context in the unattended ear. *Cognition* 1: 359–372.

Langdon-Davies, J. 1956. What is the agent's role in ESP? *Journal of the Society for Psychical Research* 38: 329–337.

Lazarus, R. S., and McCleary, R. A. 1951. Autonomic discrimination without awareness: A study of subception. *Psychological Review* 58: 113–122.

Lindsay, P. H., and Norman, D. A. 1977. *Human Information Processing: An Introduction to Psychology*, 2d ed. New York: Academic Press.

McCloskey, M., and Watkins, M. J. 1978. The seeing-more-than-is-there phenomenon: Implications for the locus of iconic storage. *Journal of Experimental Psychology: Human Perception and Performance* 4: 553–564.

MacFarland, J. D., and George, R. W. 1937. Extra-sensory perception of normal and distorted symbols. *Journal of Parapsychology* 1: 93–101.

Mackay, D. G. 1973. Aspects of the theory of comprehension, memory and attention. *Quarterly Journal of Experimental Psychology* 25: 22–40.

McMahan, E. A. 1947. A PK experiment under light and dark conditions. *Journal of Parapsychology* 11: 46–54.

Maher, M., and Schmeidler, G. R. 1977. Cerebral lateralization effects in ESP processing. *Journal of the American Society for Psychical Research* 71: 261–271.

Markwick, B. 1978. The Soal-Goldney experiments with Basil Shackleton: New evidence of data manipulation. *Proceedings of the Society for Psychical Research* 56: 250–277.

Marshall, N. 1960. ESP and memory: A physical theory. *British Journal for the Philosophy of Science* 10: 265–286.

Mewhort, D. J. K.; Merikle, P. M.; and Bryden, M. P. 1969. On the transfer from iconic to short-term memory. *Journal of Experimental Psychology* 81:89–94.

Millar, K. 1975. Processing capacity requirements of stimulus encoding. *Acta Psychologica* 39: 393–410.

Mischo, J., and Weis, R. 1973. A pilot study on the relations between PK scores and personality variables. In *Research in Parapsychology 1972*, W. G. Roll, R. L. Morris and J. D. Morris (eds.). Metuchen, N.J.: Scarecrow Press.

Moncrieff, M. M. 1951. *The Clairvoyant Theory of Perception.* London: Faber & Faber.

Nash, C. B., and Nash, C. S. 1963. Comparison of responses to ESP and subliminal targets. *International Journal of Parapsychology* 5: 293–307.

Nash, C. S., and Nash, C. B. 1968. Effect of target selection, field dependence, and body concept on ESP performance. *Journal of Parapsychology* 32: 248–257.

Neisser, U. 1967. *Cognitive Psychology.* New York: Appleton-Century-Crofts.

Norman, D. A. 1976. *Memory and Attention: An Introduction to Human Information Processing,* 2d ed. New York: Wiley.

Orme, J. E. 1974. Precognition and time. *Journal of the Society for Psychical Research* 47:351–365.

Osgood, C. E.; Suci, G. J.; and Tannenbaum, P. H. 1957. *The Measurement of Meaning.* Urbana: University of Illinois Press.

Owen, A. R. G. 1964. *Can We Explain the Poltergeist?* New York: Garrett Publications.

Paivio, A. 1971. *Imagery and Verbal Processes.* New York: Holt, Rinehart & Winston.

Palmer, J. 1971. Scoring in ESP tests as a function of belief in ESP. Part I. The sheep-goat effect. *Journal of the American Society for Psychical Research* 65: 373–408.

Palmer, J. 1972. Scoring in ESP tests as a function of belief in ESP. Part II. Beyond the sheep-goat effect. *Journal of the American Society for Psychical Research* 66: 1–26.

Persinger, M. A. 1974. *The Paranormal. Part I. Patterns.* New York: MSS Information Corp.

Persinger, M. A. 1975. ELF waves and ESP. *New Horizons* 1 (5): 232–235.

Posner, M. I., and Mitchell, R. F. 1967. Chronometric analysis of classification. *Psychological Review* 74: 392–409.

Postman, L. 1975. Verbal learning and memory. *Annual Review of Psychology* 26: 291–335.

Pratt, J. G., and Keil, H. H. J. 1973. Firsthand observations of Nina S. Kulagina suggestive of PK upon static objects. *Journal of the American Society for Psychical Research* 67: 381–390.

Pratt, J. G.; Rhine, J. B.; Smith, B. M.; Stuart, C. E.; and Greenwood, J. A. 1940. *Extra-Sensory Perception after Sixty Years: A Critical Appraisal of the Research in Extra-Sensory Perception.* New York: Holt.

Pratt, J. G., and Woodruff, J. L. 1939. Size of stimulus symbols in extrasensory perception. *Journal of Parapsychology* 3: 121–158.

Pratt, J. G., and Woodruff, J. L. 1946. An exploratory investigation of PK position effects. *Journal of Parapsychology* 10: 197–207.

Price, H. H. 1940. Some philosophical questions about telepathy and clairvoyance. *Philosophy* 15: 363–385.

Price, H. H. 1964. Memory and paranormal cognition. *Journal of Parapsychology* 28: 300–301. (An abstract.)

Puthoff, H. E., and Targ, R. 1976. A perceptual channel for information transfer over kilometer distances: Historical perspective and recent research. *Proceedings of the Institute of Electrical and Electronics Engineers* 64: 329–354.

Pylyshyn, Z. W. 1973. What the mind's eye tells the mind's brain: A critique of mental imagery. *Psychological Bulletin* 80: 1–24.

Randall, J. L. 1975. *Parapsychology and the Nature of Life.* London: Souvenir Press.

Rao, K. R. 1966. *Experimental Parapsychology: A Review and Interpretation.* Springfield, Ill.: Thomas.

Rao, K. R. 1977. On the nature of psi: An examination of some attempts to explain ESP and PK. *Journal of Parapsychology* 41: 294–351.

Rao, K. R.; Morrison, M.; Davis, J. W.; and Freeman, J. A. 1977. The role of association in memory-recall and ESP. *Journal of Parapsychology* 41: 190–197.

Rhine, J. B. 1969. Position effects in psi test results. *Journal of. Parapsychology* 33: 136–157.

Rhine, L. E. 1953. Subjective forms of spontaneous psi experiences. *Journal of Parapsychology* 17: 77–114.

Rhine, L. E. 1954. Frequency of types of experience in spontaneous precognition. *Journal of Parapsychology* 18: 93–123.

Rhine, L. E. 1962. Psychological processes in ESP experiences. Part I. Waking experiences. *Journal of Parapsychology* 26: 88–111.

Rhine, L. E. 1963. Spontaneous physical effects and the psi process. *Journal of Parapsychology* 27: 84–122.

Rhine, L. E. 1976. *Psi: What Is It?* New York: Harper & Row.

Rhine, L. E., and Rhine, J. B. 1943. The psychokinetic effect. I. The first experiment. *Journal of Parapsychology* 7: 20–43.

Richardson, A. 1977. Verbalizer-visualizer: A cognitive style dimension. *Journal of Mental Imagery* 1: 109–126.

Roll, W. G. 1966. ESP and memory. *International Journal of Neuropsychiatry* 2: 505–521.

Ryzl, M. 1970. *Parapsychology: A Scientific Approach.* New York: Hawthorn.

Sakitt, B. 1976. Iconic memory. *Psychological Review* 83: 257–276.

Schechter, E. I. 1977. Nonintentional ESP: A review and replication. *Journal of the American Society for Psychical Research* 71: 337–374.

Schechter, R.; Solfvin, G.; and McCollum, R. 1975. Psi and mental imagery. *Journal of the American Society for Psychical Research* 69: 321–326.

Scherer, W. B. 1948. Spontaneity as a factor in ESP. *Journal of Parapsychology* 12: 126–147.

Schmeidler, G. R. 1961. Evidence for two kinds of telepathy. *International Journal of Parapsychology* 3: 5–48.

Schmeidler, G. R. 1962. ESP and tests of perception. *Journal of the American Society for Psychical Research* 56: 48–51.

Schmidt, H. 1970. PK experiments with animals as subjects. *Journal of Parapsychology* 34: 255–261.

Schmidt, H. 1974. Comparison of PK action on two different random number generators. *Journal of Parapsychology* 38: 47–55.

Schmidt, H. 1976. PK effect on pre-recorded targets. *Journal of the American Society for Psychical Research* 70: 267–291.

Schouten, S. A. 1976. Autonomic psychophysiological reactions to sensory and emotive stimuli in a psi experiment. *European Journal of Parapsychology* 1 (2): 57–71.

Schroder, H. M., and Suedfeld, P. (eds.). 1971. *Personality Theory and Information Processing*. New York: Ronald Press.

Schwarz, B. E. 1967. Possible telesomatic reactions. *Journal of the Medical Society of New Jersey* 64: 600–603.

Segal, S. J., and Fusella, V. 1970 Influence of imaged pictures and sounds on detection of visual and auditory signals. *Journal of Experimental Psychology* 83: 458–464.

Sheehan, P. W. 1967. A shortened form of Betts' Questionnaire upon Mental Imagery. *Journal of Clinical Psychology* 23: 386–389.

Shwartz, S. P. 1976. Capacity limitations in human information processing. *Memory & Cognition* 4: 763–768.

Simon, H. A. 1979. Information processing models of cognition. *Annual Review of Psychology* 30: 363–396.

Sinclair, U. 1962. *Mental Radio,* 2d ed. Springfield, Ill.: Thomas.

Smith, G. J. W., and Henriksson, M. 1955. The effect on an established percept of a perceptual process beyond awareness. *Acta Psychologica* 11: 346–355.

Soal, S. G., and Bateman, F. 1950. Agents in opposition and conjunction. *Journal of Parapsychology* 14: 168–192.

Spelke, E.; Hirst, W.; and Neisser, U. 1976. Skills of divided attention. *Cognition* 4: 215–230.

Sperling, G. 1960. The information available in brief visual presentations. *Psychological Monographs* 74 (11, whole no. 498).

Sperling, G. 1963. A model for visual memory tasks. *Human Factors* 5: 19–31.

Spinelli, E. 1977. The effects of a cognitive task on children's GESP abilities. Paper presented at the (first) International Conference of the Society for Psychical Research, London, April 14–17.

Stanford, R. G. 1969. "Associative activation of the unconscious" and "visualization" as methods for influencing the PK target. *Journal of the American Society for Psychical Research* 63: 338–351.

Stanford, R. G. 1974a. An experimentally testable model for spontaneous psi events. I. Extrasensory events. *Journal of the American Society for Psychical Research* 68: 34–57.

Stanford, R. G. 1974b. An experimentally testable model for spontaneous psi events. II. Psychokinetic events. *Journal of the American Society for Psychical Research* 68: 321–356.

Stanford, R. G. 1974c. Correspondence: Dr. Stanford's reply to Dr. Schmeidler's letter. *Journal of the American Society for Psychical Research* 68: 444–446.

Stanford, R. G. 1977. Experimental psychokinesis: A review from diverse perspectives. In *Handbook of Parapsychology*, B. B. Wolman (ed.). New York: Van Nostrand Reinhold.

Stanford, R. G. 1978. Toward reinterpreting psi events. *Journal of the American Society for Psychical Research* 72: 197–214.

Stanford, R. G., and Fox, C. 1975. An effect of release of effort in a psychokinetic task. In *Research in Parapsychology 1974*, J. D. Morris, W. G. Roll and R. L. Morris (eds.). Metuchen, N.J.: Scarecrow Press.

Stanford, R. G.; Zenhausern, R.; Taylor, A.; and Dwyer, M. A. 1975. Psychokinesis as psi-mediated instrumental response. *Journal of the American Society for Psychical Research* 69: 127–133.

Steen, D. 1957. Success with complex targets in a PK baseball game. *Journal of Parapsychology* 21: 133–146.

Stevenson, I. 1970. Telepathic impressions: A review and report of thirty-five new cases. *Proceedings of the American Society for Psychical Research* 29: 1–198.

Tart, C. T. 1963. Physiological correlates of psi cognition. *International Journal of Parapsychology* 5: 375–386.

Tart, C. T. 1966. Models for the explanation of extrasensory perception. *International Journal of Neuropsychiatry* 2: 488–504.

Taylor, J. 1975. *Superminds: An Investigation into the Paranormal*. London: Macmillan.

Taylor, J. 1978. Personal communication, May 10.

Tenhaeff, W. H. C. 1972. *Telepathy and Clairvoyance: Views of Some Little Investigated Capabilities of Man.* Springfield, Ill.: Thomas.

Thalbourne, M. 1978. An improved method of analyzing free-response material. Paper presented at the Second International Conference of the Society for Psychical Research, Cambridge, England, March 28–30.

Theios, J. 1975. The components of response latency in simple human information processing tasks. In *Attention and Performance*, vol. 5., P. M. A. Rabbitt and S. Dornic (eds.). London: Academic Press.

Ullman, M.; Krippner, S.; with Vaughan, A. 1973. *Dream Telepathy.* New York: Macmillan.

Underwood, B. J. 1969. Attributes of memory. *Psychological Review* 76: 559–573.

von Wright, J. M. 1970. On selection in visual immediate memory. *Acta Psychologica* 33: 280–292.

Warcollier, R. 1938. *Experimental Telepathy.* Boston: Boston Society for Psychic Research.

Warcollier, R. 1948. *Mind to Mind.* New York: Creative Age Press.

Warr, P. B. (ed.). 1970. *Thought and Personality: Selected Readings.* Harmondsworth, England: Penguin.

Weiskrantz, L.; Warrington, E. K.; Sanders, M. D.; and Marshall, J. 1974. Visual capacity in the hemianopic field following a restricted occipital ablation. *Brain* 97: 709–728.

Wertheimer, M. 1958. Principles of perceptual organization. In *Readings in Perception*, D. C. Beardslee and M. Wertheimer (eds.). Princeton, N.J.: Van Nostrand.

White, R. A. 1964. A comparison of old and new methods of response to targets in ESP experiments. *Journal of the American Society for Psychical Research* 58: 21–56.

White, R. A. 1976. The influence of persons other than the experimenter on the subject's scores in psi experiments. *Journal of the American Society for Psychical Research* 70: 133–166.

Wickens, D. D. 1972. Characteristics of word encoding. In *Coding Processes in Human Memory*, A. W. Melton and E. Martin (eds.). Washington, D.C.: Winston.

Wickens, D. D. 1975. Personal communication, August 11.

Wiklund, N. 1975. Aftereffect perception, preconscious perception, and ESP. *Journal of Parapsychology* 39: 106–119.

Witkin, H. A. 1965. Psychological differentiation and forms of pathology. *Journal of Abnormal Psychology* 70: 317–336.

Witkin, H. A.; Dyk, R. B.; Faterson, H. F.; Goodenough, D. R.; and Karp, S. A. 1962. *Psychological Differentiation: Studies of Development.* New York: Wiley.

Witkin, H. A.; Lewis, H. B.; Hertzman, M.; Machover, K.; Meissner, P. B.; and Wapner, S. 1954. *Personality through Perception: An Experimental and Clinical Study.* New York: Harper.

Worthington, A. G. 1964. Differential rates of dark adaptation to "taboo" and "neutral" stimuli. *Canadian Journal of Psychology* 18: 257–265.

Zotti, E., and Cohen, D. B. 1970. Effect of an ESP transmitter vs. a non-ESP transmitter in telepathy. *Journal of Parapsychology* 34: 232–233. (An abstract.)

AUTHOR INDEX

SUBJECT INDEX

Activity dimension 29

Afferent features 10, 18, 19, 20, 22, 23, 24, 25

Afferent processing 10, 18–19, 21, 55
  and ESP 65, 67, 74–75, 84, 93–94

Afferent storage 10, 19–21, 23, 25, 54, 55, 97

Agent, telepathic 125–127, 131–132, 135–137

Agnosia, visual 70

Ambiguous input 30–31, 35

Analytic mode 48–49

Arousal, level of
  and ESP 132–133, 136–137
  and PK 140–144

Attention 12, 31, 35, 55–60, 128–129
  and consciousness 38, 58–59
  and ESP 65, 108, 111
  and practice 59, 133
  and semantic analysis 58–59
  and the sense organs 17

Attitude to ESP 65, 69

Automatisms 104, 133

Betts' QMI 99

"Blind sight" 19

Bottom-up processing *see* Flow of information

Brain damage 70

Breadth of processing 31, 34, 38, 49

Capacity for processing *see* Processing capacity

Capacity interference 56–57, 134

Capacity theory 56–57, 128–129

Causal direction 123, 126

Cerebral hemispheres
  and ESP 101
  and PK 119

Chunking 35

Clairaudience 91

Clairvoyance 2, 6, 77, 78, 84, 86, 95, 96

Coding *see* Encoding

Cognitive control processes 12, 14–16, 17, 22, 24, 29, 35, 36, 38, 47, 48, 56–59, 74, 124, 128

Cognitive style 47–51, 53
  and ESP 100, 111, 112
  and PK 119–120

Collective unconscious 79, 81

Competing agents 131–132

Complexity of task 129–130, 138–139

Components, systemic (*see also* Processing loci) v, 9, Ch 2, 60

Concordance 106, 107, 108, 117, 123, 124, 126, 127, 135–136, 146

Concreteness 36

Conformance 106, 117

Confusion matrices 96–97

Connotative features 29–30
  and ESP 92, 102–103, 111

Consciousness (*see also* States of consciousness) 11, 18, 30, 31, 33, 37–38, 58–59
  and ESP 3, 64, 67–68, 70, 71, 75, 80, 81, 92, 93, 98, 102, 103, 104, 107, 111–112, 134, 135
  and PK 120, 121, 124, 125

Context (*see also* Expectations) 24, 46, 110

Control processes *see* Cognitive control processes